Managing Your Child's Chronic Pain

Managing Your Child's Chronic Pain

TONYA M. PALERMO, PhD

EMILY F. LAW, PhD

OXFORD
UNIVERSITY PRESS

OXFORD

UNIVERSITY PRESS

Oxford University Press is a department of the University of
Oxford. It furthers the University's objective of excellence in research,
scholarship, and education by publishing worldwide.

Oxford   New York
Auckland   Cape Town   Dar es Salaam   Hong Kong   Karachi
Kuala Lumpur   Madrid   Melbourne   Mexico City   Nairobi
New Delhi   Shanghai   Taipei   Toronto

With offices in
Argentina   Austria   Brazil   Chile   Czech Republic   France   Greece
Guatemala   Hungary   Italy   Japan   Poland   Portugal   Singapore
South Korea   Switzerland   Thailand   Turkey   Ukraine   Vietnam

Oxford is a registered trademark of Oxford University Press
in the UK and certain other countries.

Published in the United States of America by
Oxford University Press
198 Madison Avenue, New York, NY 10016

© Oxford University Press 2015

Library of Congress Cataloging-in-Publication Data
Tonya M. Palermo
Managing your child's chronic pain / Tonya M. Palermo, Ph.D., Emily F. Law, Ph.D.
   pages cm
Includes bibliographical references and index.
ISBN 978–0–19–933004–1 (paperback)
1. Pain in children—Treatment—Popular works.   2. Chronic pain—Treatment—Popular
works.   3. Cognitive therapy for children—Popular works.   I. Law, Emily F.   II. Title.
RJ365.P383 2015
618.92'0472—dc23
2014044320

9 8 7 6 5 4 3
Printed in the United States of America
on acid-free paper

To Tom, Isabella, Amelia, and Luca (TMP)
To Andy and Asher (EFL)

Contents

Preface

"Life is going to pass us by unless we learn how to cope and take charge."
    —*Mother of a 15-year-old with chronic musculoskeletal pain*

Although people all over the world have chronic pain, there are only a small number of healthcare providers who have expertise in how to help people with this problem, especially children and adolescents. Most of these healthcare providers work in specialized pediatric pain clinics in children's hospitals. Unfortunately, there are very few of these pediatric pain clinics around the globe. This means that many families are not able to get the help they need because they live too far away from a treatment center. We have written this book to help address this problem. It provides access to effective and easy-to-do psychological treatment strategies that parents can use themselves to help their children and families better cope with pain.

Together, we share a wealth of experience in providing and studying psychological treatments for children and adolescents with chronic pain. Dr. Tonya Palermo is a pediatric psychologist and an internationally recognized expert in the assessment and treatment of chronic pain in children and adolescents. She has over 20 years of experience providing treatment to children with chronic pain and to their parents, and she has worked in several different pediatric pain clinics in the United States. Dr. Palermo also has an active research program funded by the National Institutes of Health that is focused on understanding the impact of chronic pain on children and their families. She also develops and evaluates cognitive-behavioral pain management treatments for children with chronic pain. Dr. Emily Law is a pediatric psychologist with experience in studying pain and treating children with chronic pain. She provides services to children and their families in the outpatient pediatric pain clinic and intensive pain rehabilitation program at Seattle Children's Hospital. Dr. Law completed a fellowship in pediatric pain research under the mentorship of Dr. Palermo. Together, we continue to collaborate on research examining cognitive-behavioral treatments for children with chronic pain and their families. We share a passion for ensuring that all children with chronic pain have access to high-quality care for pain.

Our approach to writing this book was to recreate the work we do in person with families. By offering this information and instruction in a self-help book, we hope to provide parents of children with chronic pain access to effective cognitive-behavioral treatment strategies that they can put into practice themselves (a description of cognitive-behavioral treatment and what it means is provided in the Introduction). We think these strategies will be easy for most parents to implement, simply by following the instructions we provide in this book. The chapters that follow provide information about pain and pain treatment. They contain detailed instruction in cognitive-behavioral strategies to help your child reduce his or her pain and participate more in important activities like going to school and social events. We also provide instruction on strategies that may help you to reduce your own stress, model positive coping methods for your child, and help your whole family adjust to the challenges of supporting a child with chronic pain. The book also teaches strategies to help with other problems your child may be experiencing, such as difficulties with sleep, attending school, staying physically active, maintaining friendships, and developing independence.

Over the years, we have learned that the participation of parents and caregivers in children's pain treatment is vitally important. Parents are the ones who are at home each day to support the use of helpful pain coping strategies. Parents also serve as their children's most important daily role models for how to approach life's challenges. We have also learned that caring for a child with chronic pain can be stressful and leaves many parents feeling helpless. Therefore, we devote a number of chapters to strategies that parents can use to help reduce their own stress so that they can better support their children's pain management.

Through this book, you will learn a range of cognitive-behavioral skills to help treat your child's chronic pain. The reason that cognitive-behavioral skills are so important to learn is that they can lead to lifelong changes. While other treatments (such as medications) may provide short-term relief, they carry a risk of serious side effects. Many of these other treatments have also not yet been rigorously studied to determine whether or not they are likely to benefit your child. By contrast, cognitive-behavioral skills for pain management provide an important nonpharmacological approach that has no side effects, can be easily learned, and has been rigorously studied for many years. There is strong evidence that cognitive-behavioral therapy is an effective treatment for children with chronic pain. The skills in this book can help your child manage pain. Practice of these skills may also lead to long-standing changes in your family's ability to cope with stress and live a healthy lifestyle.

We recommend that you try *all* of the skills described in each chapter so that you find the ones that are most effective for you and your family. We find that it is best to try the skills in each chapter for at least a week or two before moving on to the next chapter. It can take some time for you to determine whether or not a particular skill is a good fit for your family. It may be simplest to focus on only one or two skills at a time so that you can take the time necessary to determine which skills work for you.

Many parents have told us that they have never met another family with a child who has chronic pain. This book also includes the "voices" of real children and parents to help remind you that you are not alone. We describe actual cases from our clinical practices and offer quotes from children with chronic pain and their parents throughout the book (the stories are real, but we have changed all names and identifying information to protect their identities). We hope that you can relate to the experiences of these other families who have coped with chronic pain.

We use the term "children" to refer to young children under 10 years of age, pre-teens, and teenagers. But when issues are specific to one age group, we use the terms "young children" or "older children and adolescents."

The cognitive-behavioral treatment strategies in this book have already helped hundreds of children and teens with many types of pain problems to have less pain and to be able to participate more in daily activities such as school, sports, and spending time with friends. Families have improved their communication, decreased conflict, and found helpful ways to support their children's coping with pain. Parents have reduced their own stress, felt less impacted by their children's chronic pain, and experienced fewer negative emotions. We sincerely hope that you and your family find the strategies presented in this book just as useful.

Tonya M. Palermo, Ph.D.
Professor, Anesthesiology and Pain Medicine
Adjunct Professor, Pediatrics and Psychiatry
University of Washington and Seattle Children's Hospital

Emily F. Law, Ph.D.
Assistant Professor, Anesthesiology and Pain Medicine
University of Washington and Seattle Children's Hospital

Acknowledgments

The inspiration for writing this book came directly from the many families who we have had the pleasure of working with over the years in different pain clinics. We thank all of these children and parents for sharing their stories (many did so specifically for this book) and for teaching us about living with chronic pain. You are the reason for this book. You have given us motivation to develop effective treatments to help parents and families better cope with chronic pain.

Writing this book also required time and understanding from our own families. Fortunately, we have the continuous encouragement of our spouses and children, who gracefully support the blending of family and work endeavors. Our own wonderful children have taught us firsthand about the joys and challenges of parenting; they have also helped us in experimenting with the parenting strategies that we share in this book.

Writing this book also required support. We sincerely thank Andy Law for his excellent assistance in carefully editing the chapters. We also thank our colleagues at Seattle Children's Hospital for their support and enthusiasm, and particularly Gaby Tai, for her help with collating and formatting the chapters.

Managing Your Child's Chronic Pain

Introduction

Madeline is a 15-year-old girl with abdominal pain and headaches that occur most days of the week. Because of her pain, she has missed 99 days of school this year and is no longer able to play volleyball. Her parents have taken her to see a number of specialists and she has tried many different medications, but she has not experienced any improvement in her pain.

IN THIS INTRODUCTORY CHAPTER WE DESCRIBE THE PURPOSE OF the book and how to get the most from it. You will also learn about chronic pain and the different reasons why children may have pain. We describe cognitive and behavioral strategies for pain management and how these skills can make a positive difference.

What is Cognitive-Behavioral Therapy?

Cognitive-behavioral therapy (CBT) is a form of psychotherapy that emphasizes the important role of thoughts and behaviors in how we feel and what we do. While there are different types of CBT, they all have similar approaches that focus on how to change the way we think in order to feel better and act differently, even if the situation itself does not change. CBT is usually a brief therapy completed in 10 sessions or less, is instructive (for example, it teaches a person how to perform a specific strategy or skill), and uses homework assignments and practice to encourage rapid learning. CBT has nothing to do with "just talking"; it is not a "talk therapy." CBT is goal oriented—that is, the person sets goals that he or she wants to achieve and works toward them in treatment. CBT is also a type of self-management therapy. This means that a person learns a skill to use to manage his or her own condition, instead of a therapist or clinician doing something to the person. Because it is a self-management approach, it can be easily learned.

Cognitive-Behavioral Therapy Is . . .

- Brief—usually completed in 10 or fewer sessions
- Instructive (teaches a specific strategy or skill)
- Goal oriented
- Empowering—teaches people to manage their own conditions independently
- Not "talk therapy"

How to Use this Book

You are most likely a parent or caregiver, family member, or friend, who is reading this book because a child you care about has chronic pain. This book will teach you about chronic pain and instruct you in cognitive and behavioral strategies for helping the child in your life who is struggling with pain.

This is what sets our book apart from others. Many books about chronic pain only provide information. We want to go beyond giving you information. We want to teach you to use effective strategies that will make positive changes in your child's life and in your family. From this book, you will learn many of the strategies taught by psychologists working in specialized pediatric pain clinics. We provide instructions on how to talk with your child about each skill. We would like you to view yourself as your child's coach as you teach him or her the pain coping skills you will learn from this book.

View yourself as your child's coach as you teach him or her the pain coping skills you will learn from this book.

In each chapter we present information about different cognitive and behavioral strategies and skills. Then we offer opportunities to practice these skills. These assignments are an important part of the book, as they are designed to give you a way to learn the skills by doing them so that you can see how they work for you.

Remember, when it comes to learning CBT skills, "It's a marathon, not a sprint." This book should not be read in one sitting. The skills take time to learn and are best learned by having many practice opportunities. Because it is so important to have time to do each assignment (like trying a certain new skill for several weeks), we recommend that you spend at least a month or two going through the chapters and carrying out the assignments.

Our book is also comprehensive, covering all the major skills with which children and families who are coping with chronic pain may need help. You will also learn about

- The common struggles that families of children with chronic pain face,
- The importance of getting good support,
- Using relaxation strategies,
- Reward systems,
- Supporting sleep and healthy lifestyle habits, and
- Improving communication.

However, each chapter can also serve as a resource for learning about one particular type of skill (for example, relaxation skills). So if you have already received instruction in other strategies and just want to learn a particular new skill, you can go straight to that chapter.

What Is Chronic Pain?

Although it is a complex problem, chronic pain has a surprisingly nonspecific definition. *Chronic pain* refers to pain that has lasted for at least 3 or 6 months. This time period was chosen (by professionals who work in the field of pain management) because it is the amount of time that would be expected for someone to recover from an illness, injury, or surgical procedure. Therefore, if a child has pain that has lasted for over 3 or 6 months, that pain would be considered chronic pain.

Chronic pain is different for each child. Pain may be mild or extremely intense. Pain may be there every day or may come and go. Pain may also be from a chronic disease (such as cancer or neurofibromatosis). For other children, the pain condition is the problem all by itself (such as functional abdominal pain), and there is no medical diagnosis to explain it.

Chronic pain is very common. Studies show that about 25% of children and teenagers (that is, 1 in 4) have some type of problem with chronic pain. The most common types of pain that children experience are head pain, abdominal pain, and musculoskeletal pain. More girls than boys have chronic pain, especially after puberty. The peak age at which chronic pain is reported in childhood is ages 14–15 years. A smaller number of children (about 5–10%) will have pain that is severe and frequent enough that it begins to limit their participation in activities, such as sports, and going to school. To put this in perspective, these figures suggest that more children have chronic pain than have most other common medical conditions, such as diabetes or asthma.

About 25% of children and teenagers (that is, 1 in 4) have some type of problem with chronic pain.

So, if pain is so common in children, why don't we hear more about it? Pain is a symptom (not a diagnosis), and so there are many different types of doctors that evaluate pain. For example, gastroenterologists (GI doctors) most often evaluate children with stomach pain; a neurologist will evaluate a child with headaches; and other specialists will evaluate children according to the location and type of pain the child has. Therefore, the management of pain gets distributed among different areas of healthcare. And, because there are fewer children living with chronic pain than the total number of adults with chronic pain, we hear more about the impact of chronic pain on adults. We will get back to these points later.

Common Pain Conditions in Children

Children can have pain in virtually every bodily location. The most common pain conditions experienced by children and adolescents are muscle pain, abdominal pain, and headaches.

Musculoskeletal Pain

Musculoskeletal pain (muscle pain) may be experienced as aching muscles, joint pain, sharp, stabbing pains, or burning pain. There are many causes of musculoskeletal pain. Children may have a rheumatological condition like arthritis that causes muscle and joint pain, or they may have developed muscle pain after an injury. Muscle pain can also occur when a child's body becomes deconditioned from lack of activity.

Abdominal Pain

Abdominal (stomach) pain is also common in children. This might involve pain in the abdomen or other gastrointestinal symptoms like nausea, vomiting, bloating, constipation, or diarrhea. Abdominal pain is treated differently when the child has a diagnosis of a chronic inflammatory condition (a structural problem in their bowel), such as inflammatory bowel disease or Crohn's disease. These children will need to take medications to control the inflammation. This is not to be confused with irritable bowel syndrome, which is a common condition that does not involve any structural problem or disease process.

Headaches

Headache pain is also frequent among young people. Headaches in childhood are most likely to be recurrent tension headaches or migraine headaches. Headaches may occur once in a while or may be present most days. The term *chronic daily headache* refers to headaches that are present on more than 15 days per month. Some children have other symptoms with headaches, such as nausea, vomiting, or sensitivity to light or sound.

Other Pain Conditions

Other pain conditions that less commonly occur in children include neuropathic pain, fibromyalgia, and disease-related pain. The word *neuropathic* refers to a nerve-type pain that is often experienced as burning or shooting pain. One kind of neuropathic pain found in children is complex regional pain syndrome, type 1 (CRPS). The reason this condition develops is poorly understood; the pain usually follows a minor injury and often involves the arms or legs. Children with CRPS often stop moving the affected body part, which can lead to limited range of motion. These children may also experience changes in skin color in the affected area. CRPS can be very difficult for physicians to diagnose—it is rare and they may have never treated a child with this condition before. Previously, this condition was referred to as reflex sympathetic dystrophy (RSD). In some parts of the world this condition is called reflex neurovascular dystrophy (RND), although this is not the proper term for the diagnosis. We present these terms here because many parents have told us they are confused about the various terms used for this condition.

Fibromyalgia syndrome (FMS) is a disease characterized by widespread pain in the fibrous tissues of the muscles, ligaments, and tendons. The diagnosis is made by examination of trigger or pressure points on the body that are very painful for people with this condition. In addition to pain in most of the body, people with fibromyalgia often have sleep problems. While fibromyalgia is more common in adults, it can also occur in children. It is sometimes referred to as "chronic widespread pain." Other terms that may be used by pain professionals to describe chronic pain that is widespread include "central sensitization" and "amplified pain syndrome." Although these are not medical diagnoses, they describe the more generalized phenomenon of changes in pain processing (in the brain) that seem to occur with chronic pain. We will describe this processing in greater detail later, in our discussion of the differences between acute and chronic pain.

Pain Related to Chronic Health Conditions

Children may also experience pain from a chronic health condition. Many children with chronic conditions have pain from medical procedures, and some children will have pain most days from their disease. For example, children with sickle cell disease, cancer, inflammatory bowel disease, and neurodegenerative diseases (i.e., diseases in which there is loss of neurological function due to abnormalities in the nervous system, such as encephalopathies) often experience pain. Pain may be a symptom of the condition or may be caused by the treatment of the condition (for example, surgery or medications). Most children with cancer experience some pain. Children may have musculoskeletal pain related to the location of a tumor, or they may develop neuropathic pain from receiving certain chemotherapy (e.g., vincristine).

Many children with chronic conditions have pain from medical procedures, and some children will have pain most days from their disease.

Similarities Among All Chronic Pain Conditions

Although children can have many different pain conditions, there are numerous ways in which all chronic pain conditions are similar. Chronic pain of any type has a similar impact on the lives of children and their families. Pain can affect children's participation in physical, social, and recreational activities, as well as their school attendance and performance. Pain can also affect parents and families by creating worries, stress, and financial burden. You will read more about the impact of pain on families in Chapter 1.

Another way that chronic pain conditions are similar is that they all place children at risk for experiencing chronic pain in adulthood. Studies have shown that children who experience chronic pain are more likely to have pain in adulthood than are children who grow up without chronic pain. Lastly, as we describe later in this chapter, similar strategies are used to evaluate and treat children with different types of pain conditions. That is why, in this book, we have focused on general cognitive and behavioral strategies that can help children with *any* type of chronic pain.

Understanding Chronic Pain

There are many reasons for pain persisting or becoming chronic. For example, your child's biology and physiology, mood and psychological functioning, and social environment can all play a role. Scientists have also discovered that the experience of having pain for a long time can change how the brain processes pain. These discoveries have led researchers in the field of pain management to understand pain more like a chronic disease than as a symptom.

What Is the Difference Between Acute Pain and Chronic Pain?

Everyone has experienced acute, everyday pain. Acute pain serves a very useful purpose. Acute pain signals that there is an injury, an infection, or inflammation that needs immediate attention. For example, a child who complains of ear pain may have an ear infection. Acute pain is like an alarm telling you that you need to take some action, such as pulling your foot away after stepping on something sharp.

Chronic pain is different. Chronic pain often does not serve any useful signaling purpose. This type of pain may or may not mean that there is damage in the body. For some people, chronic pain is not caused by an illness. In this case, chronic pain can be like a false alarm, because pain nerves send pain signals to the brain, even though there may be nothing wrong with the bones, muscles, or other parts of the body that the signal is coming from. We know that for some children, pain signals continue even when no acute injury or tissue damage is present. This is due to some of the changes that happen in the brain, in the pain-processing pathways that lead to pain sensitivity in broad areas of the body. In the medical literature this phenomenon is referred to as "central sensitization."

> Chronic pain can be like a false alarm, because pain nerves send pain signals to the brain, even though there may be nothing wrong with the bones, muscles, or other parts of the body that the signal is coming from.

It can be hard for people without chronic pain to understand the experience of chronic pain because they can't see it. Although your child is experiencing a real physical sensation, there may be no external signs, such as a broken bone or a cast. Even though doctors may have run tests on your child and they come back "normal," this does not mean that the pain isn't real. Children who have chronic pain are not pretending, even if it seems like there is no physical reason for them to have pain. This is part of why chronic pain is puzzling; it can be hard to understand the child's experience.

Stories from Families Like Yours

"Our story began with a snowball effect. Jessica's pain started with a cold. Strange, I know, however one thing led to another. A cold turned into another cold, into another illness, and then into back pain. She has scoliosis. Then doctors found a ruptured cyst on an ovary, and she had more back pain. . . . she spiraled out of control! We spent more time at doctor appointments then she did at school. She became "stressed" as well as the rest of the household. She was an above-average student and she was missing so much school that her grades failed. Jessica started having more stress, which led to more pain. Her pain was so bad that she could not concentrate in school. She couldn't sit, she couldn't stand, and she couldn't lie down. She was diagnosed with chronic pain. We tried several different things. She tried pain medications . . . no relief; she tried physical therapy . . . no relief . . . she tried acupuncture . . . no relief . . . she tried biofeedback, some relief."

—*Alice, mother of 15-year-old Jessica*

Why Does Chronic Pain Develop?

So if chronic pain does not always mean there is an urgent problem in the body, then why does it develop? Scientists have been studying the development of chronic pain for a number of years, and those who treat children and adults with chronic pain now understand the condition through what is called the *biopsychosocial model of pain*. The biopsychosocial model explains how a child's biology and genetics (*bio*), psychological functioning (*psycho*), and social environment (*social*) can all play a role in the pain condition. We will talk about each of these areas next.

Studies have shown that some types of pain conditions run in families. This means that your child may have been born with a tendency to experience a pain problem. One example of this is migraine headaches: Children are more likely to experience migraines if someone in their family has had migraines. This doesn't mean that your child is destined to be in pain, but this pattern does show that your child's *genetics* may have contributed to a pain problem.

Another reason for pain developing is children's *physiology* and the physical demands placed on their bodies. For example, some children have a lot of mobility in their joints, and when they participate in certain activities they may experience frequent joint dislocations and pain. Or, a child may also have a medical condition that affects his or her physiology; for instance, children who have arthritis often experience pain in their joints. Children who are undergoing treatment for cancer may have pain from the chemotherapy they are taking (as a side effect) or from the disease and its location, such as a bone tumor.

"Maggie feels angry, doesn't understand why this has happened to her. She sometimes blames me because of my personal problems with pain (fibromyalgia)—the possible heredity (genetic) part of her condition."

—*Diana, mother of 15-year-old Maggie*

Other reasons that chronic pain may develop have to do with children's *psychological functioning*, or their mood and emotions. Studies have shown that having negative emotions like anger, sadness, worry, and disgust is related to experiencing higher levels of pain. Parts of the brain related to the perception of pain are also involved in the regulation of emotion. This means that changes in the brain that occur with processing of pain may also have an effect on your child's emotions (and vice versa). Coping with any difficult symptom is harder when a person experiences negative emotions. Some children feel that "constant pain impacts every waking minute." They may feel embarrassment, worry, fear, resentment, anger, and agitation. This doesn't mean that these negative emotions *caused* the pain but that they may be an important part of what is making it difficult for the child to cope now.

There are also reasons for pain continuing over long periods of time that have to do with the *social environment* surrounding a child. Social factors, such as how caregivers, teachers, and friends respond to the child in pain, can play a role in how children cope. For example, for some children being able to stay home (from school and other activities) feels easier and less stressful and has positive aspects.

Unfortunately, however, a pattern can develop in which children do not have enough "push" to get back into their usual activities. In these situations, changes may need to be made in the social environment in order to help the child better cope with pain. In Chapter 4, we provide suggestions for motivating your child to cope positively with pain, through the use of reward systems.

Pain Primer: How Is Pain Experienced in the Body?

Pain is a physical sensation that is controlled by the brain. When you experience an acute injury (like touching a hot burner with your hand), the nerves in your hand transmit a chemical and electrical message to nerves in the spinal cord. These connect with other nerves and send the message to your brain that you have hurt your hand. This is called the *pain pathway*. The brain then takes this message and tells you that your hand hurts, so you shout, "Ouch!" The pain message is then sent back through the pathway from your spine to your hand. All of this happens very quickly.

In some types of chronic pain conditions, researchers believe, nerves continue to send pain messages to the brain even when there is no local inflammation or injury. This means that even when the hand is no longer on the hot plate, the chemical and electrical message is still sent to nerves and communicated to the brain. It is like a faulty message to the brain exclaiming "danger" when there really is no problem with the muscles or tissues. Research has shown that many things impact the strength and experience of pain signals. This work may provide clues as to how to best treat chronic pain.

For example, changes in the body can increase pain signals. These changes may include loss of sleep (sleep deprivation), tense muscles, less or more activity than normal, and feeling anxious and worried. On the other hand, research has also shown that pain signals can be blocked or reduced by relaxation, distraction, and positive feelings.

What Are Cognitive and Behavioral Strategies for Pain?

Cognitive and behavioral strategies refer to techniques for teaching people how to manage pain by learning new ways to think about the pain and change behaviors related to the pain. Knowing that pain is a

Cognitive and behavioral strategies can alter pain signals and change how pain is experienced.

physical experience, you may wonder why cognitive and behavioral strategies would be useful for pain management. There are a number of reasons why these strategies are useful for producing long-term changes in a person's pain experience. First, these strategies target the areas in the brain that are involved in pain perception. Pain signals activate areas of the brain that deal with memory, emotions, understanding, and sensation. Because activities in the different areas of the brain contribute to the experience of pain, cognitive and behavioral strategies can alter pain signals and change how pain is experienced. Second, changing behavior is the best way to make long-term changes. By learning how to perform activities despite having pain and to cope better with challenges related to pain, your child will gain skills important to his or her health and well-being.

These methods may provide long-lasting changes for your child, and the skills can stay with the child for the rest of his or her life. Your child's thoughts, behaviors, emotions, and social environment affect the pain, but he or she can learn new patterns and skills that can reduce pain signals and change the impact that pain has on daily life. As a parent or caregiver, the skills and management techniques you learn will help to improve your child's functioning and help your child feel supported in his or her efforts to cope with pain.

Cognitive-behavioral therapy has been used for over 30 years as an intervention for children with chronic pain. Behavioral strategies include learning of the following types of skills:

- Deep breathing and relaxation training
- Strategies to manage sleep problems
- Reward systems (e.g., teaching strategies to parents to reinforce and reward adaptive behaviors, such as school attendance)
- Strategies to increase physical activity

Cognitive strategies include

- Learning skills to manage stress,
- Skills to improve communication and relationships, and
- Learning to think in new ways (cognitive coping skills).

CBT programs contain a mix of behavioral and cognitive strategies. Formal CBT programs are often led by mental health experts, either individually or in groups. But as noted in the Preface to this book, not everyone has access to such programs. That is why, in the chapters that follow, we provide instruction in using CBT strategies yourself.

How Effective are CBT Programs?

CBT has been studied among children for treatment of many different pain conditions (e.g., migraine, abdominal pain, fibromyalgia). It has been found to be effective in reducing children's pain and in helping to restore children's ability to function in their daily lives. The findings from recent studies show that one in two children benefit from CBT treatment. In fact, compared to other treatments, such as medications, physical therapy, and complementary and alternative therapies (e.g., acupuncture), there is much more evidence supporting the effectiveness of CBT. CBT is considered appropriate for children and adolescents with any chronic pain condition, including disease-related pain.

Summary

Chronic pain is a common problem in children and adolescents. Across Europe and North America, similar rates of chronic pain have been reported, with about 5–10% of children experiencing severe and debilitating pain. We know that the most common childhood pain is headache, abdominal pain, and musculoskeletal pain, and that girls are affected more than boys. Chronic pain can have a tremendous impact on children's everyday life. CBT is an effective treatment for chronic pain and has strong supporting evidence for helping children with many different pain conditions. This book will teach you several cognitive and behavioral strategies that you can use to help your child cope with pain.

How Pain Affects Children and Families

For the past 6 months, Emma has been experiencing persistent headaches, from when she wakes up in the morning until she falls asleep at night. Emma is beginning to have problems with attending school, completing her school work, and participating in sports and extracurricular activities. She also feels like other kids don't understand what she's going through, and this has been stressful and caused more worries. Emma's parents are very upset and want to do whatever is necessary to get pain relief for their daughter.

THE GOAL OF THIS CHAPTER IS TO EXPLORE THE DIFFERENT WAYS IN which chronic pain can have an impact on children, parents, and the whole family. Some of these may be true for your family, and others may not. We highlight these experiences so that you can see you are not alone; many other families have gone through the same experiences. Fortunately, the strategies in this book have helped many of these families cope better with chronic pain.

We also will discuss how to recognize signs of depression and anxiety in children and offer strategies that you can use to help your family cope. Parental self-care, family routines, and social support are all important to coping with chronic pain.

How Pain May Affect Children

Some children with pain symptoms have very little disruption in their day-to-day lives. They keep going to school, playing sports, and spending time with friends. It may be that these children have less severe pain or that they are able to cope with it more readily than other children with chronic pain. Children may also push themselves to continue with their activities because they don't want to have their lives impacted by pain. Some children want to hide their pain from others. Other children with pain symptoms have major disruption in their daily lives. Every child responds differently, even to severe pain.

Having pain for a long time can also affect how children feel. In general, children with chronic pain experience more stress than do other children. They can also feel less cheerful and have more worries compared to children without pain. In some children, significant problems with anxiety or depression might develop that require separate treatment by a mental health professional. It is important to understand that pain is an unpleasant experience for everyone, and too many negative feelings can get in the way of recovery.

"Despite being optimistic on most days, [our daughter] becomes agitated and very frustrated trying to live through the pain and is very, very tired of feeling sick. She feels she has the right to feel this way, as anyone would in her shoes. She does not get to live life the way she has expected, and trying to change her expectations and limitations has been challenging."
—*Kris, mother of 16-year-old Minna, who has chronic widespread pain*

Recognizing Signs of Depression and Anxiety

Parents often ask how to spot signs of more serious depression and anxiety in their kids. This can sometimes be difficult for parents, especially when their children are more introverted. We advise parents to focus on the following areas to help decide whether evaluation and treatment for depression or anxiety may be necessary.

Signs of Depression

- Your child does not seem to be enjoying any of his or her usual interests.
- Your child mostly wants to be alone and has given up on the majority of the things he or she used to enjoy.
- Your child's mood seems extremely negative or hopeless.
- Your child is voicing thoughts about hurting him- or herself. (If this is the case, you must obtain a mental health evaluation immediately. Your priority must be to protect your child's safety.)

Signs of Anxiety

- Your child responds to situations with nervousness or tries to avoid certain activities or situations.
- Your child is not able to separate from you easily.
- Your child exhibits a great deal of worry or concern about regular daily events.

If any of these scenarios sound familiar, have a conversation with your child about his or her feelings. Ask your child how he or she is dealing with things. If you are concerned about your child's level of distress or the intensity or quality of mood, it is important that you share this concern with your child's healthcare providers so that your child can receive appropriate treatment.

Pain can also interfere with a child's ability to get a good night's sleep. Being in pain can make it tough for people to fall asleep and to sleep comfortably for an adequate period of time. We know that many children with chronic pain have sleep problems. Unfortunately, not getting enough good-quality sleep can make it hard for children to feel their best during the day and to participate fully in activities. In Chapter 6 we talk more about children's sleep and strategies to address difficulties falling asleep or staying asleep.

For many children, school performance is affected by pain. School represents the "daily work" of children, but those with chronic pain may have problems going to school or staying in school all day. They can also have problems concentrating and completing their schoolwork. Difficulties at school are stressful for most children and can affect their mood. This in turn can increase stress levels for the whole family. School is such an important issue for families coping with chronic pain that we have devoted an entire chapter to this topic (see Chapter 7).

Effects on Parents and Families

When a child is having difficulties with pain, it can affect parents and the whole family in different ways. Parents have their own emotional responses to the diagnosis and management of their child's chronic pain. You may be discouraged by a lack of clear diagnosis or treatment plan. You may experience anger, worries, or fears about your child's condition. Parents can also feel powerless to help their child in pain. These emotional responses can create additional stress for parents and within the family. Sometimes the stress can result in more arguments and conflict and less family harmony.

"When severe enough, the pain causes her to have to disrupt what she is doing, like marching band or in the classroom. Last year this caused her to struggle to get caught up, which made things worse. But we are going into the new school year much more educated and she has adjusted her schedule to not be as stressful."

—*Wendy, mother of 13-year-old Ciara, who has chronic abdominal pain*

In addition, family time is impacted by chronic pain. Dealing with chronic pain may be a very time-consuming process involving multiple doctors' appointments, long drives or flights to treatment centers, and searching for information online or at the library. Devoting this much time to having a child's pain evaluated and treated can change family routines. It may make it difficult to spend time with other children and to devote time to other pursuits, such as spending time with friends, a partner, and in community activities.

Parents may also experience the financial burden of the evaluation and management of chronic pain. This might include uncovered charges for diagnostic exams, medications, and treatments. In addition, parents may have to bear costs related to taking time off from work, transportation, and additional childcare for siblings. As Tariq, father of a 12-year-old with neuropathic pain, said, "Families who have a child dealing with chronic pain have so much to juggle: Doctor visits regularly—numerous weekly (some out of state); therapies—numerous weekly; other children, et cetera." Altogether, managing the tasks related to parenting a child or adolescent with chronic pain is a significant challenge.

> "At this time my daughter's pain controls her life. It also affects many things in the family's life. For example, we didn't get to have a family vacation this summer and it is difficult to travel even for the weekend. We worry that it will continue to control our lives for a long time."
> —*Susan, mother of a 13-year-old with pain related to Charcot-Marie Tooth disease*

Sibling Reactions

"I get so annoyed that Mandy asks me constantly to get stuff for her ('bring me my cell phone, bring me my charger, bring me a glass of water.') She treats me like her slave," says Amelia, whose sister has chronic musculoskeletal pain. Siblings can also be affected by changes in schedules and priorities and in the overall family tempo. Siblings may feel left out as their parents spend increased time with their brother or sister with chronic pain. They may also feel jealous of the extra attention that their brother or sister receives. Sometimes, as with Amelia, siblings get angry at negative behavioral changes in their brother or sister with chronic pain. Siblings may also worry about their brother or sister, or about the extra stress their parents are experiencing. When a child has chronic pain, the whole family can be affected.

Searching for Answers

Many parents are concerned that their child's pain means that he or she has a medical problem that has not yet been identified. They worry that something is being missed. They may have heard a story from a friend or family member about a similar problem, and get ideas about possible diagnoses or tests that should be performed. Some parents search for medical information on the Internet or at the library. Parents may feel strongly that a cure for the pain can be found, with enough searching.

In our experience, it is harder for families of children with chronic pain to focus on recovery when they are still searching for a diagnosis. It might feel frustrating to accept that "chronic pain" itself *is* the diagnosis. However, chronic pain is very common, much more common than many diseases in childhood. Although some children will go through a long evaluation process and eventually be diagnosed with a rare illness, this is highly unusual.

On the other hand, as a parent you do need assurance that the proper evaluations have been conducted for your child. Most children with chronic pain have been seen by many specialists and have tried many different medications and other treatments, often over several years. It can be hard to recognize that there is an end point. For parents who are beginning to learn CBT strategies for addressing their child's chronic pain, we encourage them to take a step back and get some overall perspective on the pain problem. It can be helpful to ask for a frank discussion with the child's pediatrician (without the child being present) to review where the family is at with evaluation and treatment of the chronic pain problem. This conversation can help families place some limits on "cure-seeking." For you as a parent, this means that your family will be empowered to focus fully on your child's

"Our family is working well, I think, through the transition to learning to 'manage' my daughter's chronic condition, instead of 'waiting' for a cure to happen."

—Robert, father of a 15-year-old with chronic widespread pain recovery. In order for CBT to be effective, you will need to focus on recovery.

You may also feel discouraged because the treatments offered to your child are not working, or because you feel you are being told that your child's pain isn't real. This can be extremely frustrating for both you and your child. As Carol, whose 16-year-old daughter has chronic jaw pain, told us, "I think she is frustrated with people (doctors included) telling her that nothing is wrong, that we don't have a conclusive reason for the pain. I think she's disappointed that the medicines aren't making her better." Parents may become desperate to have their child's pain relieved.

It can also be challenging to figure out where to go for quality pain care, and you may struggle with getting insurance coverage for treatment. Many pain centers have long wait times for an appointment, so even when you have figured out where to go to get treatment for your child, it is not unusual to have to wait 3 or 4 months for an appointment. We will review information about the range of treatments you may be seeking for your child's chronic pain, in Chapter 2.

How Has Pain Impacted Your Child and Family?

Chronic pain is a difficult experience for everyone involved. Your child has been dealing with his or her own challenges, and in turn, the pain may have affected your family. Sometimes there is more of an impact than anyone realizes. It is also possible that you and your family are coping well and have managed to deal effectively with the many stresses. Table 1.1 lists some common problems that parents have told us they've experienced when their child has chronic pain. As you read this list, think about the problems you and your family deal with. In Chapter 2 you will be asked to develop goals for working on your child's pain management, so keep in mind the problems that you identified from this list, because they may help you come up with your own goals for using the CBT strategies in this book.

TABLE 1.1 Common Problems in Families Coping with Chronic Pain

Child Function and Behavior
- ☐ I can't get my child to go to school or to other activities.
- ☐ My child won't do his physical therapy.
- ☐ My child doesn't leave the house anymore.
- ☐ I'm worried my child won't have any friends.
- ☐ I'm worried my child won't graduate from high school.
- ☐ I can't get my child to do chores.

Parent Distress
- ☐ I worry more than ever now.
- ☐ I can't seem to think straight.
- ☐ I have problems making decisions.
- ☐ I have difficulty talking to my friends.
- ☐ Most of my friends shun me.
- ☐ I worry about how much to push my child.
- ☐ I'm worried that my child will never get better.
- ☐ I think I'm a terrible parent because I should be able to help my child.
- ☐ I can't take much more of this.
- ☐ I don't have any time to myself.
- ☐ I feel helpless.
- ☐ My life feels like it is falling apart.
- ☐ I feel sad all the time.
- ☐ I have trouble sleeping.

Family and Marital Issues
- ☐ Treating my child's pain is becoming a financial burden.
- ☐ I'm worried I'm going to lose my job.
- ☐ Our family doesn't get along well any more.
- ☐ We aren't talking a lot lately.
- ☐ This situation is putting strain on my marriage.
- ☐ I have no time for my other children and my spouse.
- ☐ There is too little affection between us.
- ☐ There is a change in family roles.

Interactions with Healthcare or School System
- ☐ I can't get the information I want.
- ☐ I can't seem to communicate with the medical team.
- ☐ I can't seem to communicate with the school staff.
- ☐ I get nervous asking questions.
- ☐ I don't like feeling out of control.
- ☐ I get very angry waiting for so long to talk to the doctor for just a few minutes.

Strategies for Coping as a Family

In this section, we describe three strategies that can help the whole family cope better with the stress of chronic pain. These strategies are as follows:

- Maintaining family routines
- Getting social support
- Parent self-care

Maintaining Family Routines

"My parents never do anything that they used to with me. I used to go on bike rides with my dad—we haven't done that in forever," says Owen, whose 12-year-old sister has migraines. Over the course of dealing with your child's chronic pain problem, a number of changes may have occurred in how your family spends time. While less time may be available to spend with the other children in the family, parents need to let siblings know that they are still special and important. This includes both the words you say to them as well as your actions in the time you spend together. Think about how you can continue to give each child the time and attention that he or she needs. We recommend that parents carve out time (this might be as little as 10–15 minutes a day) to really focus on each child.

Similarly, it is important for you to find at least short times now and then to spend alone together with your partner. This might be a "date night" or simply grocery shopping together without the children. The time alone is essential to continuing to nurture your relationship during this stressful experience.

We also recommend that you find routines that can continue despite dealing with the chronic pain. Maybe your family had a Friday movie night, a Sunday brunch tradition, or a Wednesday church activity. Sometimes family routines are abandoned because a child has been ill, but with some ingenuity families are often able to find ways to make these events a family priority. This can lift spirits in the family and serve as a useful reminder that many things are possible even with the pain problem. You can also consider involving friends and extended family members in these routines, perhaps by hosting a potluck meal on a weekly or monthly basis.

"I had quit my job to stay home with Andy when his pain problem first started. But after a year we had too many financial pressures and I needed to go back to work. I felt really guilty about leaving him home alone even though he is 15 years old and capable of being by himself. Now I realize it was an important step for our family for me to go back to work."
—*Eve, whose son has chronic abdominal pain*

Another source of stress for parents is dealing with employment demands and managing family time. Parents may feel torn about taking time away from work to care for their child with chronic pain. They may face financial stress. They may use all their sick and vacation time to care for their child's needs and not be able to use any other paid time off. To deal with these challenges, some parents may take a leave from their job (such as through the Family Medical Leave Act in the United States), and some may even leave their job permanently.

However, in general, we encourage parents to maintain normal routines, including fitting in the normal demands of work. As you learn strategies to encourage your child with chronic pain to carry out his or her usual activities (such as going to school), it is helpful for you to also prioritize the demands in your life that need attention.

Social Support

When most of us hear that a person has chronic pain, the image that comes to mind is most likely of a middle-aged man or woman with back pain. We do not picture a child. As such, chronic pain is not a health problem that other parents talk about, and it is unusual for a parent of a child with chronic pain to know other families who have gone through similar struggles. Therefore, many parents (and children) feel alone, isolated, and without support.

It is important to arrange opportunities to obtain support from family and friends, though these may not occur as naturally as you would like given the time you spend on demands related to your child's pain problem. You will need to schedule time to stay connected with those close to you. This means saying "yes" to invitations from others and initiating your own invitations. You may need to alter activities (e.g., maybe you can't go out to lunch but you can have a friend stop by for a quick cup of coffee) in order for them to fit with the increased demands on your schedule. These types of opportunities can provide you with outlets for discussing your feelings. It can also lead to direct forms of support (e.g., helping with practical tasks) and can improve your mood.

You may need to decide how much information you want to communicate about your child's condition. Because chronic pain is not well understood by others, friends and family members may not grasp the situation fully. It may be helpful to talk to your child's pain doctor(s) about how to explain the pain problem to others. Most often though, it simply means that you need to be comfortable with repeating yourself, explaining something that is difficult, and taking the time needed to convey the situation so that friends or family members can understand what you are going through. Ultimately, your goal should be to ensure that those close to you understand your feelings and what your family is going through even if they don't understand everything about the pain condition.

> "Having faith in God and support around us from church friends has made a world of difference because my daughter feels like she matters."
> —*Pam, mother of 10-year-old Bailey, who has chronic neck pain*

Parent Self-Care

Parents who are taking care of a child with a chronic condition also need to take the time and make the effort to care for themselves. Parents who take care of themselves may be better able to handle the stress and challenges of caring for their children. Research has shown that when parents are depressed and having difficulties coping, their children are more likely to also have difficulties coping. So it is important for parents to focus on self-care during this time. This includes developing healthy lifestyle habits, allowing people to help the family, and staying positive.

Parents may expend so much energy toward helping their child in pain that they don't take time to engage in their own healthy lifestyles. Meals may be obtained more often while on the road (e.g., drive-thru fast food) to and from doctor's appointments, and less time may be available for important activities such as exercise. Stress related to the child's pain condition might also impact parents' moods. Increased worries can lead to sleep loss. It is important to pay attention to developing or maintaining healthy lifestyle habits, which can go a long way toward helping you feel better and able to tackle the many challenges of your child's pain problem. As a mother of a 13-year-old son, Gabriel, with pain related to a bone tumor told us, "Running is the one thing that I do that is only for me. It reduces my stress level and helps me face the day." You will learn more about supporting your child's healthy lifestyle habits in Chapter 5, but we encourage you to begin with attending to your own healthy lifestyle.

Also, it is important to let people know how difficult it is to balance all the demands of taking care of your child while he or she is struggling with this pain problem. Let people help you. Sometimes it may seem easier to do everything yourself because making arrangements with others can feel burdensome. If you are a parent to multiple children, you know well that it is a struggle to balance time and attention in the family. But when a child has a health condition, this is even harder. Accepting offers to transport children to school and sports or music practices or to bring by a nutritious meal can be just the boost you need on days when you are feeling overwhelmed. The next time a kind offer like this comes your way, say "yes."

Keeping a positive tempo in the family is also a useful strategy during this unpredictable time. As mentioned, it is very easy to feel frustrated with a lack of progress in pain management; chronic pain is a challenging problem to treat. Your child will sense your level of frustration and likely feel the same way. It will also be hard to try new pain management strategies if no one in the family expects them to be helpful. Keep an open mind, and remember that many other children

"One thing that I noticed when I got frustrated with Evan's pain not getting better is that I became really irritable and negative. I made a huge effort to put on a game face in front of Evan and my daughter, to look and sound happier, so that they didn't get down about everything too. It really helped and it made me start to feel better too."

—*Rita, whose 13-year-old has chronic back pain*

with chronic pain have made major strides in managing their pain. They have been able to decrease the pain and to get their lives back together. Show your child that you expect her or him to improve and that you will be there to support these positive changes. You will learn more about strategies for staying positive in Chapter 8.

Summary

In this chapter we discussed how chronic pain can affect virtually all aspects of a child's life. It can also impact many areas of family life. There are many common challenges that all families coping with chronic pain experience. You are not alone in this experience; change is possible. Some important strategies for parents and caregivers to work on are maintaining a healthy lifestyle, getting support from others, and practicing self-care.

Chapter 1 Practice Assignment

Your assignment for this week is to choose one self-care activity and give it a try. This might mean exercising or spending time with a friend. Your self-care activity should be one that is desirable to you, and you may need to make special arrangements to schedule this activity. To help increase your commitment to the activity, we encourage you to write it down so it is visible to you and others.

This week, my self-care activity is: _____

I will make the following arrangements to do this activity:

_____

_____

_____

_____

Getting Help and Setting Goals

Carly has chronic headaches related to her VP shunt. She sees a pediatric neurologist for her shunt and has recently been evaluated in a pain program. Carly has set several goals for herself for pain treatment. She wants to feel happier and less stressed, wants to reduce stress between herself and her parents, and wants to get to school at least 3 days per week. Carly's parents want to learn better ways to communicate with Carly so that they can support her and encourage her to engage in positive behaviors.

IN THIS CHAPTER WE WILL REVIEW THE TYPES OF PAIN TREATMENT available to children with chronic pain, and help you select goals for improving your and your child's management of chronic pain using well-tested CBT strategies. Most often, a team of professionals from different backgrounds provides chronic pain treatment for children. This means that along with cognitive-behavioral treatment provided by a psychologist, children will often be engaged in treatments with other healthcare professionals. We discuss how to stay in communication with the different providers who may work with your child and how to integrate goals from different treatments. The chapter ends with activities designed to help you select goals to pursue using the CBT strategies presented in this book.

Chronic Pain Treatment

Chronic pain is a significant health problem for many children. It is also a puzzling condition for many families. Often the phrase "chronic pain" is used by medical professionals after all other diagnoses have been ruled out. This means that affected children may have undergone many evaluations and visited many different treatment facilities. Frustratingly, a diagnosis of chronic pain may not answer the question that families have been struggling with: "What is causing my child's pain?"

The diagnosis of chronic pain also may not lead to a specific treatment to address the problem. The diagnosis and treatment of chronic pain is, in fact, different from other medical problems like asthma, cancer, or diabetes, for which there are tests and evaluations to indicate a specific diagnosis and treatment (e.g., medications or surgery).

Although our primary focus in this book is on psychological treatment and the use of CBT, it can be helpful to consider how this treatment approach may fit into the bigger picture of getting help for your child's pain problem. It is beyond the scope of this book to review all available treatments for chronic pain and the evidence to support their use with children. For more comprehensive descriptions of a broad range of pain treatments, we refer you to the Resources and Bibliography section at the end of the book.

Here we review the different sources from which you may be getting help (e.g., your child's pediatrician, specialty providers) and how to integrate goals from all treatments with CBT strategies.

Your Child's Primary Care Provider

Most often when children have significant pain symptoms parents seek the advice of their child's pediatrician or primary care provider. Ideally, this physician has knowledge of your child's history from prior well-child and sickness-related visits and you have a relationship with this physician. Because your child's primary care provider may know your family well, this person may serve as an important source of ongoing guidance and support during your child's pain evaluation and treatment. If your child's primary care provider has experience treating children with chronic pain, he or she may make recommendations for specific treatments for your child's condition.

Other times, a primary care physician will coordinate referrals for evaluation and treatment but will not directly provide management.

Regardless of what additional providers your child ends up working with, it is helpful to continue to have ongoing contact with your child's primary care provider through scheduling periodic follow-up visits to check in and discuss progress. In this way, one individual (your child's primary care provider) can talk with you about the various evaluations and can assist your family in sorting through the complexities of assessment and treatment. You can ask that your child's pediatrician talk with all other providers involved in your child's care so that he or she has all of the relevant knowledge of the evaluations performed and recommendations made for treatment.

> Your child's primary care provider may serve as an important source of ongoing guidance and support during your child's pain evaluation and treatment.

Specialty and Subspecialty Care

Your child's primary care provider may have arranged for evaluations to be completed by specialty or subspecialty physicians such as a neurologist, gastroenterologist, or orthopedics specialist. The type of specialist will depend on the bodily location in which your child has pain. For example, a child with back pain may be referred to an orthopedics specialist, while a child with abdominal pain may be referred to a gastroenterologist. The consultation might be restricted to a specific diagnostic test to rule out a medical condition, or it may include ongoing treatment. For example, children with migraine headaches may be referred to a pediatric neurologist and then receive evaluation and ongoing treatment at a neurology clinic or a headache clinic. Specialty providers may make further recommendations for evaluations from other specialists such as orthopedic surgeons, child psychologists, or pediatric pain providers.

It is helpful to have open communication between all specialists involved in evaluating your child. Signing release of information forms for specialists who do not work within the same medical center can facilitate communication and sharing of information about your child. Again, as mentioned, it is important to talk with your child's primary care provider about the recommendations made by specialty providers so that he or she can help you coordinate care for your child. Working closely with your child's primary care provider can be especially helpful when multiple specialists are involved in your child's care.

Pain Programs

In some locations, a pediatric pain clinic or program is available to provide specialized care in pain management to children. This typically includes an interdisciplinary evaluation by a team that may consist of a pain physician, psychologist, physical therapist, nurse, and/or social worker. Most children come to a pain clinic after they have completed all other comprehensive evaluations recommended by the child's primary care provider and other specialists. Treatment recommendations in a pain clinic may include visits to a psychologist for CBT; visits to a physical or occupational therapist for strength training, desensitization, or overall conditioning; visits for acupuncture, biofeedback, or other complementary therapies for pain relief; or visits with a pain physician for interventional procedures or for medication management. Treatment may occur exclusively in an outpatient clinic or may occur in the hospital.

PSYCHOLOGICAL TREATMENTS

Psychological treatments are intended to help reduce pain sensations and to change situational, emotional, and behavioral factors so that children can better cope with pain. Children may receive psychological treatment from a psychologist who works within the pain clinic. Most commonly, the psychologist works both with the child, to teach him or her coping skills, and with the parents, to provide instruction in such areas as how to communicate about pain and how to use reward systems for getting children back into activities, and to offer support and guidance. Some pain programs also offer group psychological interventions to children, such as those focusing on skills in coping with pain. These groups may consist of children and adolescents with different types of chronic pain (e.g., headache, abdominal pain) and of varying ages. A group setting can provide social support to reduce isolation and build relationships among children and adolescents and their parents. The CBT strategies that you will learn in this book are very similar to what a psychologist in a pain program would use with your child and family.

The CBT strategies in this book are very similar to what a psychologist in a pain program would use with your child and family.

In many pain clinics, pain psychologists will also routinely screen children for symptoms of anxiety and depression because such symptoms are common and can impact how children cope with pain. This does not mean that anxiety or depression is the cause of your child's pain but that these symptoms can make pain worse. If you recognize signs of depression or anxiety that seem serious (as described in Chapter 1), it is important to have your child evaluated by a mental health professional. You can ask your child's pain team, specialty provider, or pediatrician for recommendations for a psychologist or mental health provider.

PHYSICAL THERAPY AND OCCUPATIONAL THERAPY

Physical therapy (PT) and occupational therapy (OT) focus primarily on improving or restoring physical function, making daily tasks and activities easier, and improving fitness level. In children with chronic pain, the most common PT interventions focus on overall fitness level and conditioning through exercise programs (this may involve stretching, weight lifting, and walking). OT interventions for children with chronic pain typically focus on making daily tasks and activities easier, such as dressing, bathing, cooking, and writing. In addition, treatments may help children to move painful body parts and improve flexibility. Other techniques may include using heat, cold, ultrasound, and electrical stimulation to reduce pain. Typically, referrals for PT and/or OT are made for children with musculoskeletal pain (widespread as well as localized musculoskeletal pain, as in complex regional pain syndrome, or CRPS). However, children with other pain conditions may benefit from PT and OT interventions as well.

MEDICATIONS AND INTERVENTIONAL PROCEDURES

Medications are used for children with chronic pain conditions, for several purposes. Medications may be prescribed in an attempt to reduce the severity of the pain, reduce inflammation, help with sleep problems, treat anxiety or depression, or treat an underlying medical condition. For example, for children with juvenile idiopathic arthritis, medications are used to reduce inflammation, which may in turn reduce pain. Similarly, patients with neuropathic pain disorders may be prescribed anticonvulsant and antidepressant medications directed at reducing neural transmission of pain (meaning the way in which the neurons in the spinal cord communicate pain signals to the brain). Opioid medications (also known as narcotics) are most commonly prescribed for pain after surgery, for pain associated with sickle cell crisis, and for cancer pain. They are used less often for chronic pain because they do not provide as much help for this type of pain.

Nerve blocks may be recommended for certain pain conditions. A nerve block involves injection of numbing medication near certain nerves to reduce pain in that specific part of the body. You may have heard of nerve blocks if you have had surgery, as they are commonly used during and after operations to control pain. Nerve blocks can also be used to manage chronic pain, although they are less commonly used for this purpose in children. Because these are highly technical procedures, nerve blocks are usually performed by anesthesiologists or interventional pain physicians.

COMPLEMENTARY AND ALTERNATIVE THERAPIES

Complementary and alternative medicine (CAM) is a term used to refer to healthcare approaches that were developed outside of mainstream Western, or conventional, medicine. These most commonly include natural products (e.g., herbs) and mind and body practices (e.g., acupuncture, yoga, tai chi). Many individuals use complementary health approaches together with conventional medicine.

Examples of CAM include acupuncture, which involves the placement of small, thin needles at specific acupuncture points in the body along a meridian, or energy field. As another example, Iyengar yoga is a form of therapeutic yoga that involves a series of asanas (body poses) and uses props, such as blankets, bolsters, blocks, and belts, to support the body. The purpose is to promote a sense of energy, relaxation, strength, balance, and flexibility.

Community Referrals

If you do not have access to a pediatric pain clinic, you may need to arrange treatment with different local community providers, including a physical or occupational therapist, practitioners of complementary and alternative therapies, and a psychologist. In general, we recommend that you visit your child's pediatrician to discuss referral options in the community, as he or she will have information about patients' experiences with these professionals, enabling you to make an informed decision about whom to contact.

Putting It All Together

Because there are different treatments that can be helpful for chronic pain, most often families work on CBT strategies while also engaged in other treatments (such as physical therapy). Throughout the book, we discuss ways to integrate other treatment goals with the goals for CBT. For example, for children who are in physical therapy, we describe in Chapter 4 how to integrate physical therapy goals into a reward system. Sometimes it is tempting for families to want to finish one treatment before starting another one (such as wanting to finish physical therapy before starting psychological treatment). However, in our experience, it is the combination of treatments that most often leads to success. We encourage you to implement CBT strategies at the same time you are using other recommended treatments for your child's chronic pain.

> We encourage you to implement CBT strategies at the same time you are using other recommended treatments for your child's chronic pain.

Using this Book for Your Child's Pain Management: Setting Goals

As discussed in the Introduction to this book, CBT for pain management is an active form of psychological treatment and has nothing to do with "just talking about problems." Instead, patients work on reaching important goals during treatment by learning new skills and applying those skills in practice opportunities (homework assignments). We want you to set goals for you and your child to work on as you use this book. Your goals should be focused on the short term (e.g., the next month) as well as on the long term (e.g., the next year), and they should also be focused on behaviors that can change. For example, over the next few weeks, you may wish to see your child use a relaxation strategy and get to school for at least half the day. Over the next year, you may wish to see that your child's pain no longer interferes with school attendance and that conflict in your family has lessened.

Many people say that their goal is pretty simple. It is just to have the pain go away. There are several reasons why we ask children and caregivers to think about making additional goals, rather than one focused only on eliminating pain. First of all, everyone experiences pain at some time in their lives, whether from everyday bumps and scrapes, medical procedures, sickness, or a chronic pain condition. Completely eliminating pain is not usually a realistic goal. However, reducing pain and learning ways to apply cognitive-behavioral strategies to decrease distress and reduce disability are often very achievable goals.

Table 2.1 provides examples of common goals that parents and children make for themselves in learning CBT for pain management.

TABLE 2.1 Examples of Common Treatment Goals for Using CBT for Pain Management

---

- Learning new ways to respond to your child when he or she is in pain
- Supporting your child's pain management efforts
- Working with school staff to help your child succeed in school
- Getting along better in your family
- Increasing the number of strategies your child can use to help manage pain
- Allowing your child more independence in managing pain on his or her own
- Increasing your child's ability to go to school and carry out other daily activities normally
- Making pain management easier and less stressful for your family

---

It is important to choose goals that are achievable and realistic. For example, if your family is constantly arguing, it might be unrealistic for you to set a goal of not arguing at all within the next week. However, it may be an achievable goal to learn a new communication strategy and to try it out in your interactions with your family over the next week. Goals should also be specific. For example, "learning new ways to respond to my child when she is in pain" is a general goal, but it is not very specific. A more specific goal might be "to remind my child to use relaxation skills when she is in pain." This is more specific because you have stated exactly what the behavior will look like (i.e., remind your child exactly what skills to use).

We also want you to think about the goals you have for any other treatments your child is engaged in. For example, if your child needs to remember to take medication or needs to participate in a home exercise program for physical therapy, these goals can be added.

For this chapter's practice assignment, we will ask that you set goals for your child's pain management. The skills in this book are meant to help you reach these goals. Specifically, in Chapters 3 to 10, you will learn the following:

- Deep breathing and relaxation strategies that can reduce pain and stress
- Behavioral strategies that can increase your child's desirable behaviors and decrease undesirable behaviors
- How to implement a point system or reward system to change behaviors
- How to model positive coping strategies for your child
- Strategies to improve your child's diet, physical activity level, and sleep habits
- Skills to improve your communication with your child
- Skills to help manage pain and increase physical activity in young children
- Strategies to solve problems and reduce anxiety and fears
- How to enable your child to have appropriate levels of independence in managing his or her pain
- Strategies to maintain the improvements that you and your child make

Not every strategy is going to work for every child or in every family. Some of the advice we offer may not be a good fit with your situation or with your family's values and preferences. We encourage you to try out the strategies in the chapters that follow and to keep an open mind. Even if you think a strategy does not apply to your child or will not be helpful, it still is worthwhile learning about the skill and trying it out. This will help you figure out which strategies work for you and your child and will give you more choices. You may also find a creative way to modify a strategy so that it works better for you.

> Even if you think a strategy does not apply to your child or will not be helpful, it still is worthwhile to learn about the skill and try it out.

Summary

In this chapter, you read a brief overview about how pediatric chronic pain is typically treated. We discussed the importance of maintaining regular contact with your child's primary care provider throughout your child's pain treatment. Lastly, we reviewed information on how to set realistic goals for CBT for pain management. You can refer back to these goals as you learn about different skills and strategies later in the book.

Chapter 2   Practice Assignment

Your assignment is to select several treatment goals that you want to work on. Follow the guidance stated earlier about selecting specific goals and dividing short-term from long-term goals. Write these goals down below, where you can find them again. We will ask you to come back to them in a few weeks to track your progress.

My short-term goals for using CBT for my child's chronic pain management are as follows:

1. _____

2. _____

3. _____

4. _____

5. _____

My long-term goals for using CBT for my child's chronic pain management are as follows:

1. _____

2. _____

3. _____

4. _____

5. _____

Relaxation Methods for Children and Teenagers

Anita is a 17-year-old girl with abdominal pain. Her pain usually flares up in the mornings before class. She drives herself to school every day, and arrives 15 minutes early so that she can do progressive muscle relaxation in her car. Just a few minutes of relaxation before starting the school day helps her to manage her pain and to stay in school for longer periods of time.

THE GOAL OF THIS CHAPTER IS FOR YOU TO LEARN WHY RELAXATION is important for children with chronic pain. You will also learn how to teach your child a few relaxation techniques that will be helpful in reducing pain and decreasing stress. Research shows that relaxation can be more effective than medication at reducing some types of pain. Relaxation methods can also help your child to increase his or her participation in daily activities. Because relaxation strategies are easy to learn for a wide age range of children (kindergarteners to teenagers), they are often some of the first pain management skills taught as part of CBT.

Teaching Pain Coping Strategies to Your Child

To successfully teach relaxation skills it's best to think of yourself as your child's coach. It is important to be supportive and not critical. Part of this process involves setting reasonable expectations. For example, it is very common for children to find that one particular pain coping skill works really well for them, while other skills are not as helpful. Likewise, some children are able to master relaxation skills right away, while others require more practice. Still other children find none of these relaxation skills to be helpful and may instead benefit from other cognitive and behavioral strategies. This is a common situation and does not mean that your child isn't trying hard enough. We recommend that you encourage your child to have an open mind as he or she tries out the skills described in this book so that your child can find the ones that work best for him or her, and that you praise your child for efforts at trying different coping strategies. You will learn more about how to use praise and positive attention in Chapter 4.

It is also important for you to have an open mind as you try the strategies in this book. Most of the skills we describe are aimed at helping parents change their thoughts and behaviors concerning their child's pain condition. Some of these strategies may work really well for you, while others may not. The goal is to try each of the strategies so that you can find the ones that work best for you and your family.

Four Relaxation Methods for Chronic Pain

Here we describe four relaxation methods that psychologists teach to children with chronic pain. These include deep breathing, progressive muscle relaxation, guided imagery, and mini-relaxation. Deep breathing involves learning to breathe deeply and slowly. Progressive muscle relaxation involves tensing and relaxing different muscle groups to help reduce muscle tension. Guided imagery is a technique that helps children shift their attention away from pain to more pleasant thoughts and sensations. Mini-relaxation is a quick relaxation method that helps children to relax in as little time as

1 minute. All of these relaxation methods are straightforward and very easy to teach to children with chronic pain.

> Relaxation methods are straightforward and very easy to teach to children with chronic pain.

We will provide you with the same scripts and strategies that psychologists use to teach these four relaxation methods to children. You can also access audio recordings of these relaxation skills online at: http://www.seattlechildrens.org/research/child-health-behavior-and-development/palermo-lab/selected-recent-publications/. The audio files can be played on a computer or downloaded onto an MP3 player or smartphone.

Why Are Relaxation Methods Important for Pain Management?

Relaxation methods can help your child to manage pain by reducing muscle tension. Chronic pain often causes people to sit, stand, or move in uncomfortable ways. Children may also spend much longer periods of time sitting or lying down than they did before they had pain. While children do this to protect the parts of their bodies that are hurting, all of this sitting, lying down, and holding of the body in different positions can lead to increased muscle tension, greater muscle weakness, and more pain. Our bodies are designed to be in motion; this is what keeps our joints, muscles, and bones flexible and strong.

School, family, and personal stressors are common for children struggling with chronic pain. Here's what some of these children have to say:

"I had a ton of makeup work at school that I had to finish for a deadline and I didn't think I could finish in time."
> —*Liam, 12-year-old with leg and arm pain*

"I had to travel overnight to a doctor appointment."
> —*Bennett, 16-year-old with abdominal pain*

"A fight with my friend caused my stressors to rise out of control, and that resulted in a lot of body pain."
> —*Ann, 14-year-old with all-over body pain*

"My back hurt a lot and I couldn't do gymnastics."
—*Kaya, 12-year-old with back pain*

"People have been calling me a faker."
—*Joshuel, 17-year-old with shoulder pain*

"I have been missing after-school practices."
—*Nathan, 16-year-old with foot pain*

"Being sick and worrying that there is something very wrong has me very stressed."
—*Ryan, 15-year-old with headache*

Relaxation skills can also help your child manage pain by reducing stress. Having chronic pain in and of itself is stressful, regardless of whatever else your child may have going on in his or her life. When we are stressed, our bodies shift into an "alerting" response and we get an extra dose of energy. This extra energy can cause our hearts to beat faster, our breathing to quicken, and our muscles to become tense. Stress and negative emotions can also increase muscle tension and lead to more severe pain.

Your child may have stress and muscle tension without even noticing it. Relaxation can help him or her feel calmer when upset, stressed, or nervous. Relaxation can also help your child feel more in control of his or her body. You may even find relaxation strategies helpful for managing your own stress, tension, or pain.

It may seem like you should be able to just tell your child to relax, but it is not that simple. Relaxation is a skill that takes practice, just like learning to play a new sport or an instrument. The more your child practices relaxation methods, the better they will work for him or her. We recommend that your child practice each skill on a daily basis. At the end of this chapter, you will learn specific tips on how to help your child practice relaxation methods.

Practice, Practice, Practice

Daily practice is very important for children learning relaxation methods. Your child will probably not notice any changes in pain the first time he or she uses these skills, and that is nothing to worry about.

Reductions in pain will only come after lots of practice. We encourage our patients to practice each relaxation skill on a daily basis for a week or two before deciding if it

Reductions in pain will only come after lots of practice.

is a method that is going to help them. Also, it is important for your child to practice these skills even if he or she is not in pain. As you read about the relaxation methods in this chapter, think about where and when your child could practice them on a daily basis.

Deep Breathing

Deep breathing is one of the best and easiest ways to relax and reduce pain. It is also a skill that is commonly used when playing wind instruments, singing, or performing yoga. There are many different names for deep breathing, including diaphragmatic breathing, abdominal breathing, and yoga complete breathing. As you might have guessed, deep breathing involves breathing slowly and deeply from the abdomen. "I use abdominal breathing when I am feeling tense and my pain factors start rising throughout my body," says Colleen, a 14-year-old with all-over body pain.

Before teaching your child the steps of deep breathing, we recommend talking with him or her about how deep breathing can help with pain. You can try saying something like the following:

Many people change the way they breathe when they are in pain. They start taking short, shallow breaths and may not even realize they are breathing differently. Shallow breathing is also one of the first signs of stress. Shallow breathing makes the heart work harder to get oxygen to all of the tissues and organs throughout the body. This extra effort by the heart can increase muscle tension, which can make pain worse. Learning how to do deep breathing can stop this cycle.

Breathing slowly and deeply increases the amount of oxygen in the body by slowing your heart rate and the pace of breathing. It is an easy way to help the body relax. Deep breathing can make you feel good and make you more aware that you are able to make changes in your body. Deep breathing can also reduce the amount of tension and pain that you feel.

Deep breathing should be a calming experience. Ask your child to let other thoughts leave the mind while he or she is practicing and to put his or her entire focus on observing breathing. Deep breathing will work best if your child practices it every day. The more your child uses deep breathing, the better it will work to reduce pain. A good goal would be for your child to practice deep breathing for a few minutes at a time several times a day.

Deep Breathing Instructions

1. Lie down on your back, knees bent. Place one hand on your chest and one on your stomach.
2. Breathe in through your nose as much as you can while you count to five. Fill your belly with air. You should feel your bottom hand move out. Your top hand on your chest should stay still. If you are having trouble seeing your belly moving in and out, lie down and place a book flat on your belly. See if you can make the book go up and down.
3. Now breathe out through your mouth, through puckered lips, letting your belly down while you count to eight. Breathe out slowly until your stomach is flat. Feel all the muscle tension flow out of your body.
4. Repeat slowly 10 times. With each breath out, notice your body beginning to feel more relaxed.

Progressive Muscle Relaxation

Progressive muscle relaxation involves tensing and relaxing different groups of muscles in the body. Start in one area, like the hands. Tense and relax your hands, and then move on (progress) to a different muscle group. Move through all of your muscle groups slowly, one at a time, tensing and relaxing as you go. Progressive muscle relaxation can help to reduce pain by easing muscle tension and helping the body to relax. Progressive muscle relaxation helps to break the cycle of pain and tension.

Before teaching your child the steps of progressive muscle relaxation, talk with him or her about how this relaxation skill can help with pain. You can try saying something like the following:

Progressive muscle relaxation helps you notice the difference between what tense and relaxed muscles feel like. If you can learn to notice when your muscles are tense, you can learn to relax these muscles, which may help make your pain lessen. The main steps of muscle relaxation are: tense, concentrate, and relax. You will start in one area, like your hands, and then move on to a different muscle group.

As with deep breathing, progressive muscle relaxation will work best if your child practices regularly. The key to practicing progressive muscle relaxation is to go through the muscle groups in a slow sequence, holding the tension for 5 to 7 seconds and then relaxing for at least 20 seconds before moving on to the next muscle group. The practice should take about 10 minutes. If your child is getting through the practices in much less time (like 5 minutes), then he or she is moving too quickly through the exercise and should slow down.

"I do the muscle tension exercise before I go to bed. It helps when I am worked up or stressed about things."
—Justin, 13-year-old with leg pain

Children age 10 and under may have some difficulty understanding instructions for tensing and relaxing different muscle groups. We often simplify instructions for younger children and make them slightly more advanced for children over 10. Instructions for progressive muscle relaxation for younger children and older children are located in Appendices A and B.

Guided Imagery

Guided imagery involves shifting attention from unpleasant thoughts or sensations (like pain) to more pleasant ones. Children can do this by using their imagination to picture being in a "happy place." Attention plays an important role in pain perception because really feeling pain requires attention to it. Guided imagery works with children as they actively pay more attention to something else (a pleasant place) and not as much to painful sensations. Guided imagery may be easier for older children and adolescents to master than for children age 9 and younger, although some younger children are very capable of using imagery.

As with the other relaxation skills, it is important to start by talking to your child about what guided imagery is and how it might help him or her. Try saying something like the following:

This is a strategy called imagery and it involves thinking about something pleasant so that your body becomes more relaxed. Thinking about something pleasant can also be a welcome distraction from pain, because it makes your brain focus on something else.

With guided imagery, you will use your imagination to picture yourself in a pleasurable place. In order for imagery to work, it is important to be as involved as possible in the scene you are creating. The more involved you are in the scene, the harder it will be to pay attention to other thoughts and sensations (like pain).

People can draw on various types of imaginary scenes in which to relax. Relaxing scenes can be anything that has a pleasant association or feels pleasant. Some people like to remember a favorite story. Others like to remember taking a trip to a favorite place. For some people, imagining a completely made-up place can be most relaxing. Imaginary scenes work best if they can be pictured easily. It should also seem pleasant or calm to the person. Imagery works better when one can imagine more details that involve all five senses: sight, sound, smell, taste, and touch.

You can encourage your child to try different types of imaginary scenes. Here are some examples:

- Being at the beach: the sounds of seagulls, the smell of the beach, the taste of salty water, the feel of the sand on your feet, and the warmth of the sun.
- A trip to an amusement park: the sounds of people enjoying the roller coasters, the sweet smell of the cotton candy machine, the buttery taste of popcorn, and a soothing breeze blowing across your face.
- Walking in a park: the sounds of birds chirping or a dog barking, the smell of grass, the crunch of leaves or gravel under your feet, and the cool shade of the trees.
- A warm and cozy place: sitting by a campfire, lying in bed under a warm blanket, holding a cup of hot cocoa, or petting

a soft, furry animal. For each of those examples, your child could think about the warmth traveling up his or her fingers and spreading to the rest of the muscles in the body.

"I imagine my special place and have a bubble bath," says 15-year-old Nicole, who has all-over body pain. To use imagery, all your child has to do is imagine a scene that feels relaxing and calm to him or her. An imagery scene should hold your child's attention for at least 5 to 7 minutes. Talk to your child about a favorite place or a time that he or she felt really comfortable and peaceful. Ask your child to describe the place:

- What is the place or scene?
- What do you see there?
- What do you hear?
- What do you smell?
- What do you taste?
- What do you touch or feel?

Instructions for a guided imagery exercise using a hot tub or hot bath as the imaginary scene can be found in Appendix C. This exercise combines muscle relaxation and imagery and is most suitable for children over the age of 10.

Mini-Relaxation

Mini-relaxation can help your child relax when he or she is short on time. The goal of mini-relaxation is for your child to quickly use skills in breathing or imagery to feel calm and reduce tension. We recommend that you teach your child this strategy only after the other relaxation skills have been mastered.

When you talk to your child about learning mini-relaxation, try saying something like the following:

Mini-relaxation works in much the same ways as deep breathing, progressive muscle relaxation, and imagery. Ideally, it helps people get relaxed in a really short time. Mini-relaxation can help you to relax in as little time as 1 minute. Like the other relaxation methods, mini-relaxation works best if you practice it every day.

The instructions for using mini-relaxation are located in Appendix D.

Encouraging Children and Adolescents to Use Relaxation Methods

Some children are really interested in learning relaxation skills and will find it easy to follow these instructions. But other children may not want to use these strategies. Talk with your child about the potential benefits of relaxation. Encourage him or her by praising any efforts and attempts that he or she makes to practice. As you know, daily practice is very important when your child is learning relaxation methods. Talk with your child about his or her daily schedule and when relaxation practice can be fit in. It is best to pick a regular time each day to practice. Many children like to practice when they get home from school and before they start on homework. Your child can also use these relaxation skills to help with falling and staying asleep at night (which will be reviewed in Chapter 6). We recommend, however, that you start practicing the skills at a time other than bedtime so that your child can be sure to get through the entire exercise without falling asleep. After the skills are mastered they can be used to improve sleep.

Once you pick a practice time, talk to your child about where he or she will practice. It is important that your child have a private, quiet place to practice in. Work with your child to pick a place where she will not be interrupted by brothers, sisters, or pets. We recommend that your child practice each strategy at least once a day for 1 or 2 weeks. It may be easiest for your child to focus on one relaxation strategy at a time during this practice period, spending 1 to 2 weeks on each skill. After a few weeks of regular practice at home, he or she can try using the relaxation methods in other places, like at school or while exercising.

"I use relaxation most of the time now even when I am not in pain. I use it at school, in the car, and at home."

—Karen, 17-year-old with abdominal pain

It is important to praise your child when you notice him or her using relaxation skills. You will learn more about using praise to encourage positive coping behaviors in Chapter 4. You can also use what we refer to as a *reward system* to encourage your child to practice relaxation methods and to positively reinforce his or her practice (also discussed in Chapter 4). Finally, you can consider modeling the use of relaxation methods by using them yourself. You will learn more about how to model positive coping behaviors in Chapter 8.

What If Relaxation Skills Don't Work for My Child?

Some of these relaxation skills may work better for your child than others. It is important that your child try each skill for at least a week or two in order to find those that work best. Your child should practice each method for a few minutes at a time.

Practicing with an audio recording can help some children to learn the skills better. You can download audio files of the relaxation methods online at: http://www.seattlechildrens.org/research/child-health-behavior-and-development/palermo-lab/selected-recent-publications/. You can also give your older child copies of the instructions for each exercise described in this chapter.

Some children may not notice any change in pain when they first start using relaxation methods, and that is okay. Encourage your child to continue practicing the skills on a daily basis for at least a week or two before deciding they are not helpful. In our experience, relaxation methods become more effective as children continue to practice them. It is also possible that your child may report feeling relaxed and less stressed but not have a reduction in pain. We still consider this success. If your child can achieve an increased sense of relaxation and have decreased stress and anxiety, he or she can experience major benefits in terms of overall well-being. And, over time, this may also help with pain management. Therefore, we would still encourage your child to continue using the relaxation methods even if he or she doesn't notice that the pain has been reduced.

If none of the relaxation skills in this chapter are appealing to your child, you can encourage him or her to explore other activities that are personally relaxing. For example, we had one patient who did not want to use relaxation methods but was willing to apply a hot pack and listen to relaxing music when he had a pain flare. Other relaxing activities include yoga, meditation, tai chi, drawing, painting, writing, or playing.

Making Time for Yourself to Practice Relaxation Skills

You may find that relaxation strategies are helpful to you as well for decreasing stress, muscle tension, or pain. Make time to practice these skills yourself. We worked with one mother whose daughter did not want to learn relaxation skills, and at first the mother was at a loss as to what to do. Over time, however, she found the relaxation skills to be helpful in managing her own stress over her daughter's pain. She realized that she was able to take better care of her daughter when she was less stressed herself. She learned the relaxation skills and set aside 15 minutes at the end of each day to practice them. She also used her relaxation skills whenever she felt worried or stressed about her daughter. Over time, she noticed that she felt calmer throughout the day. Finally, her daughter saw her using the relaxation skills, and began to show an interest in learning how to use relaxation to reduce her own stress and manage her pain.

Tips for Practicing Relaxation Methods

You can share these tips for practicing relaxation methods with your child. You can also follow these tips when you practice relaxation yourself.

1. Relaxation methods are a set of skills that you can learn with practice. Just like playing soccer or an instrument, relaxation methods will work better the more you practice them.
2. Find a comfortable place to practice. A quiet place is best. Choose a time and place to practice when other people or pets will not interrupt you.
3. Use a comfortable chair, couch, or bed where you can relax.
4. When first learning relaxation, do not practice at bedtime. You might fall asleep before finishing! You can use these methods at bedtime later on, once you have mastered the skills.
5. Keep your legs and arms uncrossed. This helps your blood circulate in a healthy way.

6. Schedule a regular time to practice every day. It is important to practice even when you are not in pain.
7. When you practice relaxation methods, your mind will often wander. When this happens, just notice that you've wandered and bring your mind back to breathing. This will get easier with practice.

Summary

In this chapter we explained how relaxation methods can help your child feel less pain and stress. We reviewed four relaxation methods: deep breathing, progressive muscle relaxation, guided imagery, and mini-relaxation. We also reviewed how to teach your child these methods and how to decide when and where your child will practice them. Relaxation methods will work better the more your child practices. It is important to practice every day, even when your child does not have pain. You will learn more about how your child can use relaxation at school in Chapter 7. You will also learn how to use relaxation to help your child's sleep, in Chapter 6. Finally, in Chapter 9, you will learn special tips on how to support young children (under age 10) in using relaxation skills.

Chapter 3   Practice Assignment

You can teach these methods to your child by sharing the audio files available online: http://www.seattlechildrens.org/research/child-health-behavior-and-development/palermo-lab/selected-recent-publications/. You can also learn these methods yourself and then show your child how to do the exercises. Once your child has learned the skills, you should expect him or her to practice without your help. If your child is young (under age 10), he or she may require more support and coaching from you at first to learn and practice the relaxation methods. In Chapter 9, we will review approaches to supporting young children in learning and using pain coping skills.

Relaxation methods will work better the more your child practices them. It is very important that your child practice these methods even when not in pain. It is best if your child practices each relaxation skill at least one time per day. When your child is first starting out with these skills, it may be easiest for him or her to focus on just one skill at a time in the daily practice. With daily practice, children may begin to notice that they can reduce the pain as they use these relaxation methods more often.

It can also be helpful to make time for yourself to practice these skills. With regular practice, you may notice that these relaxation skills help reduce your stress. If you have a pain problem, you may find that these skills help with reducing your pain as well. Think about your schedule and when you can take 10–15 minutes to practice these relaxation exercises each day. It is helpful to practice them in a quiet place that is free of distractions. Over time, you may notice that these skills work better for you the more you practice them.

It can be useful to make some notes about the relaxation strategies that you and your child try. Write down comments regarding what was helpful, such as what types of imaginary scenes your child liked.

Relaxation Strategies

- Deep breathing:

  _____

  _____

  _____

- Progressive muscle relaxation:

  _____

  _____

  _____

- Guided imagery:

  _____

  _____

  _____

- Mini-relaxation:

  _____

  _____

  _____

Praise, Attention, and Reward Systems

Caitlin is a 10-year-old girl with complex regional pain syndrome. She is participating in an intensive day treatment pain rehabilitation program and is having a hard time doing her home exercises at the end of the day. Her parents have decided to help motivate her by using a reward system that links completion of her home exercises to one of her favorite things—painting her nails. Caitlin and her parents agree that her mother will help her paint her nails a different color each evening after Caitlin completes her home exercises. Caitlin is excited about painting her nails a new color every day.

T HE GOALS OF THIS CHAPTER ARE FOR YOU TO LEARN HOW TO USE praise and attention, and to develop reward systems to help your child manage pain. Attention and praise, when used properly, will increase your child's positive coping behaviors and decrease unwanted behaviors. Reward systems, also often called star charts, sticker charts, point systems, or behavior plans, are designed to reward your child's positive coping and activity participation. You will also learn how to recruit other family members and school personnel to support your child in reaching her goals. All of these strategies can help your child cope more positively with pain and participate in activities that he or she enjoys and that are important to your child.

Basic Principles of Behavior Management

Reward systems and the proper use of praise and attention are components of what is often referred to as "behavior management." Parents have a lot of influence over their children's behavior. They can increase their child's positive coping behaviors by using praise and rewards or privileges. Parents can also decrease their child's negative or undesired behaviors by ignoring or withholding rewards or privileges in response to those negative behaviors. The strategies that can help change problematic child behaviors are based on the following guiding principles:

- Behaviors followed by positive outcomes are strengthened.
- Behaviors followed by negative outcomes are weakened.

In other words, when your child's behavior leads to rewarding consequences, he or she is more likely to repeat this behavior. When your child's behavior leads to negative or undesired consequences, he or she is less likely to repeat this behavior.

As parents know, their attention is a powerful tool for reinforcing their children's behavior. Most children will do anything to obtain their parent's attention and approval, especially when they are young, but older children or teenagers will also do a lot to receive your attention. Paying attention to a child and giving praise in response to a particular behavior will encourage more of it, whereas a response of removing attention and ignoring will discourage it.

Attention from Parents Is a Powerful Tool for Pain Management

Many parents are familiar with using praise, attention, and reward systems to improve their children's behavior, but they may not have thought about how these strategies can help with pain. In fact, parent training in behavior management skills is an important part of pain management for children; the ways in which parents and other adults respond to a child in pain can influence how he or she behaves and copes with pain.

Parents of children with chronic pain often accidentally provide reinforcement for behaviors that lead to worse coping. This usually starts out because the child is miserable and in a lot of pain. For most parents of a sick child, the natural instinct is to provide extra attention and care. In the short term, this is usually not a problem. When children are ill for a few days, they *should* receive extra attention and care. However, the problem with chronic pain is that it doesn't last for just a few days. Over a long time period, extra attention from parents can make it harder for children to get back to normal living—that is, to participate in regular, everyday activities when they do not feel well. Increasing participation in normal activities is an important part of the treatment for chronic pain.

> Over a long time period, extra attention from parents can actually make it harder for children to participate in regular, everyday activities when they do not feel well.

For example, many parents allow their children to get out of going to school, doing chores, and other activities when they complain of pain. In some families, the only one-on-one time that children get with their parents is at doctors' appointments or when parents stay home with the child instead of going to work. In other families, the child's pain becomes the primary topic of conversation between parents and the child. Over time, children may learn that complaining about pain can help them avoid undesired activities and get extra attention from their parents. This usually occurs before parents have met with a pain specialist—that is, before they know that it is safe for their children to participate in normal activities even when not feeling well.

On the flip side, attention and praise from parents can be a powerful tool to increase children's use of positive coping skills (such as relaxation methods) and their participation in activities (e.g., school, chores, or sports) that are hard for them to do because of having pain. The strategies discussed here will teach you how to use attention, praise, and reward systems to help your child get back his or her normal life.

How to Praise a Child with Chronic Pain

Praising a child when he or she behaves courageously or appropriately can change the child's behavior. While children may sometimes act like their parents' words don't matter, your child does value your opinion, especially when it is positive. You can use praise to increase any behavior you would like your child to show more often. Here are some examples of behaviors we typically encourage parents to praise:

- School attendance
- Homework completion
- Completion of home exercise program
- Attending after-school clubs or sports practices
- Doing chores
- Practicing relaxation methods

When you provide your child with praise, we recommend the following: 1) give the praise as soon as you notice the desired behavior, and 2) be clear and specific so that your child knows exactly what you liked about his or her behavior. Simply saying "good job" is not recommended. Instead, we suggest something like this: "Stefanie, you managed to get all of your homework done even though you had a headache. I am very proud of you." Here are a few more examples of specific expressions of praise from parents of children who have chronic pain:

- "I am proud that you attended school even though you did not feel well."
- "I am so pleased to see you back participating in karate."
- "It is great when you spend time with your friends."
- "Thank you for doing a really good job cleaning your room."
- "I am proud of you for walking even though you had pain."
- "I understand you didn't sleep well and are very tired. Great job getting up and going to band practice anyway."
- "I noticed that you have been practicing your relaxation exercises. You seem more relaxed and less tired. I'm proud of you for trying new ways to manage your pain."
- "I am so proud of you for pushing to stay in school even though at times it is difficult."

- "I like how you took ownership of your problem and looked for ways to resolve it yourself."
- "I know you have a headache but I appreciate when you put your laundry away."

Some parents of children with chronic pain describe the use of attention as a balancing act. They want to give their children some extra attention because of their pain problem, but they also want to be sure they help their children live their life to its fullest despite the pain. "What I tried to do was cut her a little slack," says Erin, the mother of a 14-year-old with chronic daily headaches. "We are a pretty structured family, and so we had to look at whether we needed to change that structure to allow for more downtime. We slowed down our family schedule so that she had more time to rest. But the other piece of that was not letting her completely give up. We had to help her to get out of bed, set goals, and still try to get out there and live life even though she had pain. We had to help her live her life and not say, 'Oh that's okay, just stay in bed all day.' Trying to find that balance was a real struggle."

> Some parents of children with chronic pain describe the use of attention as a balancing act.

How to Respond to Your Child's Complaints and Refusal to Do Activities

Many parents tell us that the hardest part about cognitive-behavioral therapy for pain management is changing the way that they respond to their child's complaints about pain and negative behaviors (such as groaning, grimacing, or whining). We recommend that parents ignore these complaints and negative behaviors. This goes against parents' natural instinct to provide their child with extra attention and care. However, it can go a long way in setting an expectation for better coping, including that the child will participate in normal activities even when he or she complains of pain. As a parent, this can be emotionally challenging. You may worry that you will push your child too far, or that your child will feel like you don't care about him or her. However, our years of experience with families and countless research studies show that changing the way parents respond to children's pain complaints is a powerful (and necessary) tool for helping their children to return to a normal life.

The term *pain behaviors* refers to the entire range of verbal and physical signs that your child is experiencing pain, including the following:

- Verbal complaints of pain
- Groaning
- Wincing
- Facial grimacing
- Refusal to do activities
- Refusal to move the part of their body that is hurting
- Refusal to get out of bed, stand up, or walk

When your child has pain behaviors, we recommend acknowledging this and then encouraging your child to determine what he or she can do to help him- or herself feel better. For example, "I understand you have a stomachache. What are one or two things you could try to help yourself feel better?" Our general recommendation is to give this prompt one time, and then ignore any subsequent pain behaviors. This means turning away, walking away, and generally not responding. This approach minimizes the amount of attention you are giving to your child's pain complaints. It also encourages your child to manage the pain independently.

If your child refuses to try any strategies to help mange the pain, it is okay for you to leave your child alone and give him or her the opportunity to figure out how to cope independently. For some children, it can help to create a list of coping strategies that is posted in the bedroom or kitchen. This list can be used as a reminder of what things might help when in pain. Your child can learn to go to this list for ideas rather than coming to you for help.

Learning to Respond Differently

It can be difficult to resist responding to your child's pain complaints with extra attention. Here is how some other parents accomplished this.

- "I did not directly discuss pain. Instead, I focused on what we had to do that day."
  —Eric, *father of a 12-year-old with headaches and abdominal pain*

- "I acknowledged his feelings and encouraged him to move forward."
  —*Tamra, mother of a 13-year-old with hand pain*

- "When she complained about pain, I asked her what she thought would help."
  —*Sheri, mother of a 14-year-old with back pain*

- "When she wanted to stay home because of pain, we told her she would not have TV or movies. It would be quiet rest time. She decided to go to school and made it through the day. She was proud of being able to do it."
  —*Ann, mother of a 17-year-old with hip and knee pain*

- "I told him that his homework needed to be done whether he was sick or not, but to take breaks if he needed to."
  —*Tanay, father of a 13-year-old with chest wall pain*

- "I didn't dwell on it or give him a lot of grief. I just casually told him I was busy and he would have to get up and get his own food."
  —*Ryan, father of an 11-year-old with foot pain*

Using Reward Systems for Pain Management

In combination with praise and attention, research has demonstrated that reward systems (plans in which behaviors are rewarded when a set goal is achieved) produce positive changes in children's pain symptoms and in their participation in daily activities. We recommend using a reward system when your child is having trouble following the recommendations of his or her medical team. For example, a reward system can help increase your child's motivation to attend school, help with chores, complete homework, practice relaxation methods, and engage in physical activity.

Basic Principles of Reward Systems

A successful reward system is one in which positive behaviors are followed by predictable amounts of valuable rewards. One of the most common reward systems is paid employment. When employees work for 2 hours, they can expect to receive 2 hours' worth of pay. They can exchange this pay for things they need or want. This system is motivating because the reward is valuable, and the reward cannot be attained without employees doing the positive behavior (in this case, working).

Setting up a reward system with your child very clearly identifies your expectations for various behaviors. It is common for children (and adults) to push the limits to find out what they can and cannot get away with, but laying out specific expectations makes it easier for children and teens to understand parents' expectations for their behavior. Having a system in place also means less work for parents, as the system will dictate how to respond to the child's behaviors—that is, what behaviors lead to what rewards. The plan will tell you what reward to give and when to give it.

The same general principles apply to all types of reward systems:

- Expectations need to be consistent and must be clearly communicated to the child.
- Consequences need to be provided that are dependent upon the child's performance.

For example, you could set up a reward system linking your child's school attendance to access to his or her cell phone. On days that your child goes to school, he or she can have the cell phone. On days that he or she does not go to school, the child cannot have the cell phone.

Choosing the Behaviors to Reward

As previously discussed, there are many behaviors you might like to encourage your child to engage in to help him or her manage the pain and return to a normal life. Following are some examples of behaviors that parents target in reward systems:

- School attendance
- Homework completion
- Participation in sports, clubs, or extracurricular activities
- Relaxation practice
- Spending time with friends and family
- Completion of home exercise program
- Physical exercise
- Chores
- Independent completion of self-care activities (dressing, bathing, cooking)

While there are many behaviors you might like to encourage your child to engage in, often the best place to start when using a reward system for children with chronic pain is to increase activity participation. Consider focusing on three to five activities that your child is not fully participating in because of pain.

Choosing the Rewards

Think about activities that your child enjoys, or things you know he or she would like to have. It is likely that many of the things your child enjoys doing most are privileges. You can use his or her access to one (or more) of these privileges as a reward for positive behavior. Examples are as follows:

- TV time
- Internet time
- Access to cell phone
- Access to iPad
- Eating out at restaurants
- Video game time
- Special family meals
- Special family activities
- Independent activities, such as being allowed to attend an event without a parent
- Special purchases (e.g., new video game, new makeup)

Talk with your child to determine which of these privileges are most valuable to him or her. It is important to choose rewards that will motivate your child.

Bribery vs. Rewards

Some parents ask about the difference between bribery and rewards. They may worry that providing rewards is inappropriate or that children should do as their parents ask without receiving any incentive or enticement.

Bribery occurs when you coerce a child to do something that is beneficial only to yourself and *not* to the child. For example, let's say that you are shopping at the grocery store and your child is screaming. You find this highly embarrassing. You offer your child a lollipop to stop screaming in order to end the embarrassment you are feeling. This is a bribe.

Bribery occurs when you coerce a child to do something that is beneficial only to you and not to the child; a reward occurs when you provide positive consequences for a desirable behavior.

A *reward* occurs when you provide positive consequences for a desirable behavior (defined as one that you want to increase). Most typically, parents choose behaviors that result in positive benefits for the child (such as completing homework, playing well with siblings, and going to school). Offering a child a lollipop as a reward for remembering to complete daily chores would be considered an incentive or positive motivator. Rewards help a child learn:

- What your expectations are.
- That you care about his or her behavior.
- That doing positive things for him- or herself leads to positive outcomes.

Rewards are not a crutch, or something that your child will become "addicted" to. Rewards don't need to be increased over time. In fact, rewards from parents often help children learn to reward themselves over time and to become more self-motivated.

Designing a Reward System for Young Children

There are several challenges to consider in designing reward systems for younger school-age children (age 10 and under). First, younger children will have fewer existing privileges and responsibilities than an older child or teenager. Second, younger children need more frequent rewards and will have more difficulty making the connection between their own behavior and the reward if there is a long delay. Despite these challenges, reward systems can often be easier to implement for younger children because they may have similar systems already in place with teachers, coaches, or other caregivers. Younger children also typically respond well to low- or no-cost rewards, such as spending extra one-on-one time with parents, choosing a TV show to watch as a family, doing a baking or arts-and-crafts activity with a parent, or choosing a board game or card game to play as a family. Younger children may also be motivated by rewards involving a "grab" in a prize box filled with inexpensive trinkets from a pharmacy or dollar store. It can be fun to get creative with younger children when you talk with them about the rewards that they would like to work toward.

Designing a Reward System for Teenagers

For teens who already have a lot of independence, a reward system may sound difficult or even impossible to implement. It may have been many years since you provided rewards to your teen based on his or her behavior, or you may have used privileges only as punishments rather than as rewards. For example, you may have taken away TV, phone, or video game time when your teen broke rules.

On the other hand, you may not be used to thinking about things like television, phone, or computer use as privileges because they have become so commonplace in most households. However, unlike basic necessities such as shelter, food, and water, a privilege is something that your teen does not need. Consider television. Watching television is a privilege because it is not a basic need, and parents pay for the cable, TV set, and electricity. Eating out at restaurants is a privilege because it is not a necessity, and parents pay for the meal. Think about your teen's day. What does he or she use and enjoy? What do you pay for? What things can you modify and use as rewards? As with younger children, we suggest that you talk with your teen about what rewards and privileges would be motivating. However, if your teen is not willing to engage with you in making a reward system, it is okay to start with something you know your teen likes or enjoys.

> Think about your teen's day. What does he or she use and enjoy? What do you pay for? What things can you modify and use as rewards?

You may wonder how you can modify certain privileges with an older teen (who may be used to carrying out most activities independently). Sometimes the answer is to get a little creative. For example, in one family a teenage boy with functional abdominal pain earned $10 toward refurbishing his car for every week during which he completed his physical therapy home exercise plan at least three times. In another family, a teenage girl with headaches earned a different accessory for her junior prom (e.g., shoes, hair, nails, dress) for every week that she met her goal for school attendance.

Point Systems and Privilege Systems

There are two general types of reward systems we describe here to increase children's participation in activities: a point system and a privilege system. Both of these reward systems can be used with children and teens of varying ages. However, for younger children, we recommend making the rewards more frequent and ensuring that rewards are provided as soon as possible after the desired behavior is performed.

Point Systems

The basic idea behind a point system is that the child's behavior, such as participation in an important activity like attending school, earns him or her a certain number of points that can be exchanged for rewards and privileges. The system can be designed so that daily rewards are provided, in addition to longer-term rewards that build up over time. The most important or most difficult activities or behaviors are assigned the most points, and less important or easier activities are assigned fewer points. An important activity like school attendance would be assigned the highest number of points, while less important activities, like household chores and physical exercise, could be given smaller point values.

DAVID'S POINT SYSTEM

To demonstrate the use of a point system in action, consider the example of David, a 16-year-old boy with back pain. The sample worksheets provided here list activities, point values, and goals assigned by David's parents. Prior to beginning the reward system, David's parents reviewed the worksheets with him in order to ensure his active participation. In the following example, note that:

- The expected activities are very specific (e.g. "setting the table" vs. "doing a chore").
- The point values reflect relative importance.

- Many pleasurable activities are considered "privileges." For example, getting to watch TV or talk on the phone are earned rather than automatically granted.

David's parents assigned points to each activity in which they wanted David to increase participation. They also defined daily and weekly point goals, and set daily and weekly privileges that David could earn. Notice that David has to attend at least a half-day of school and do the dishes after dinner in order to be able to play video games. He can earn daily rewards, but he can also save his daily points toward a larger, weekly goal and reward. Check out David's point system worksheet (see Table 4.1).

A simple calendar can be used to tally points and track accomplishments. An example of David's calendar is presented in Table 4.2.

Privilege Systems

A second type of reward system is the privilege system. Using this system, one important activity is selected, such as school attendance, and privileges are made contingent, that is they are dependent upon reaching a set goal. For example, if your goal for your daughter's school attendance is for her to attend a full day of school, then specific privileges are made available each day for accomplishing that, while other privileges are not made available if the goal is not reached. Rewards and privileges are directly paired with an important goal or activity each day. One consideration in using the privilege system (instead of the point system) is that only one or two important activities should be targeted.

TAMMY'S PRIVILEGE SYSTEM

To demonstrate the use of a privilege system in action, consider the example of Tammy, a 14-year-old girl with migraines. Tammy's mother developed a privilege system in which she paired cell phone access with school attendance. If Tammy attends school, she can have her cell phone. If not, then cell phone access is lost for that whole day. Another example is to pair video game access with exercise. If Tammy spends 20 minutes riding her bike, she gets 1 hour of video

TABLE 4.1 David's Point System Worksheet

Activities to Reward

David will receive points for the following activities. He is responsible for tracking these on the calendar and for adding them up at the end of the week. He can either cash in the points at the end of the day or save them for a larger reward. This system should be renegotiated every week so that activities reflect the things he is currently trying to work toward.

Activities	Points
Attending school ½ day	15
Attending school full day	25
Going to soccer practice	5
Finishing homework	10
Doing the dishes after dinner	5

Points can be exchanged as follows. Overflow points are not lost (for example, if he gets 55 in one week and exchanges 50 for a movie, he can keep the 5 for later).

Daily Point Goal: *30–40* Points

Points	Daily Privileges/Rewards
1 hour of TV or video games	20

Weekly Point Goal: *200* Points

Points	Weekly Privileges/Rewards
Going out with friends	150
Going to a movie with dad or friends	150
New video game	200+ for 2 weeks in a row

I agree to put forth my best effort to do the activities that will earn me points.

Child/Teen's Signature: David

I/We agree to follow the point system to help reward David for reaching his goals.

Parent's/Parents' Signature: Mom & Dad

TABLE 4.2 David's Calendar to Track Points

Week of: August 10	Monday	Tuesday	Wednesday	Thursday	Friday	Saturday	Sunday
Activities Completed	School (1/2 day): 15	School (1/2 day): 15	School (full day): 25	School (full day): 25	School (full day): 25	Soccer: 5	Homework: 10
	Dishes: 5	Dishes: 5	Homework: 10	Dishes: 5	Soccer: 5	Homework: 10	Dishes: 5
				Soccer: 10	Homework: 10	Dishes: 5	
	Day Total:	Day Total:	Day Total:	Day Total:	Day Total:	Day Total:	Day Total:
Total Points Earned	20	20	35	40	40	20	15
							Week Total: 190

TABLE 4.3 Tammy's Privilege System Worksheet

Tammy will receive privileges for the following activities. This system should be renegotiated every week so that activities reflect the things she is currently trying to work toward.

Activity #1	Privilege
Attend school	Cell phone access

Activity #2	Privilege
Ride bike for 20 min	1 hour of video game time

I agree to put forth my best effort to do the activities that will earn me privileges.

Child/Teen's Signature: _Tammy_

I/We agree to follow the privilege system to help reward _Tammy_ for reaching her goals.

Parent's/Parents' Signature: _Mom_

game time. If she does not ride her bike for 20 minutes, then she does not get any video game time for that day.

   Check out Tammy's privilege system worksheet in Table 4.3.

Establishing Your Own Reward System

Now that you have learned about different types of reward systems, you can use the worksheets in Appendices E and F to set up your own privilege system or point system. We also encourage you to use these worksheets when you talk about the reward system with your child or teenager.

How to Make a Point System

To make a point system, you will need to specify the activities you want your child to participate in more often, and the privileges or rewards he or she will earn for participating in those activities. You will also need to assign different point values to each activity. Next, you will need to develop daily and weekly point goals. The daily point goal represents how many points your child would need to earn every day to earn the daily reward. The weekly point goal represents how many points your child would need to earn by the end of the week to earn the weekly reward. You may consider multiplying the daily point goal by seven in order to reach the weekly point goal, or you may want to build in some flexibility and multiply the daily point goal only by five. Finally, you will need to identify the daily and weekly rewards that your teen can earn. The maximum daily points should equal your daily point goal, and your maximum weekly points should equal your weekly point goal. As you know, you can target multiple activities at the same time when you use a point system. Use the worksheet in Appendix E to set up your point system. We have also included a calendar that your family can use to track activities and points.

How to Make a Privilege System

When using a privilege system it is important to focus on only one or two activities at a time. You will need to choose the desired activity or behavior that you would like to see your child participate in more frequently. In addition, you will need to decide on the privilege(s) that you will pair the behavior or activity with. It is helpful to be highly specific in your description of the privilege (e.g., how long will cell phone access last each day?) You can use the worksheet in Appendix F to set up your privilege system.

Tips for Establishing an Effective Reward System

There are a few steps that you can take to ensure that your reward system has the best chance for success:

1. Explain the system to your child, including the specific expectations for the activity you want to reward. During this conversation, it can be very helpful to talk with your child about how you want to reward his or her hard work in the pain management program.

2. Focus on the rewards (rather than the consequences), and be sure your child has the chance to easily earn them at the beginning. Remember that you want your child to experience success, so make the goals fun and rewarding but also easy for him or her to achieve.

3. Be sure to pay close attention to details! For example, what if there is no school (i.e., a holiday)—will an alternative activity be substituted to earn privileges that day? If you are using the point system, will you allow extra points from one week to roll over into the next week? Who will record the points? If you are keeping a calendar, it should be in a visible or central location for both you and your child to see.

4. Make sure that your child and all adults in the household understand the system and agree on how it will work. Consistency in implementing the reward system is very important. The most common reason for the failure of reward systems is lack of consistency. Creating a written contract with your child and the other adult family members in your home can help everyone stick to the boundaries and expectations outlined in the reward system.

5. Avoid accidental rewards (e.g., allowing access to TV or some other reward without your child earning it), vague instructions (e.g., "You'll get 10 points if you get out and do something"), and inconsistency between parents ("Okay, I guess you can have the points for setting the table even though you only did half of it.")

6. Set reasonable expectations. Another common reason for failure of reward systems is that the goals are too hard. If your child doesn't experience any initial success or earn the rewards, then he or she won't be motivated to continue. It is important to set the expectations at a level that your child can reach, especially in the beginning. You can increase your expectations (make achieving the goals harder) over time as your child experiences more success. So for example, it may not be reasonable to expect a full day of school attendance from a teen who has not been able to do this for months, but you might ensure success if you expect 2 hours of school attendance at first and then gradually increase your expectation for the amount of time your child spends in school.

7. Be excited about success (e.g., "Awesome! You got enough points for a movie!") and matter-of-fact about failures ("Oh well, you don't quite have enough points for TV tonight."). Give your child the message that you believe that he or she can cope and can accomplish the goals.
8. Make a special time for talking with your child about how the system is working and for discussing possible improvements. As he or she increases activity participation, new goals can be added.
9. If you don't think you can take away a certain privilege, then that is not a good one to pick as part of a reward system. For example, some parents may not want to take cell phones away during the school day because it is their only way of reaching their child during and after school. However, it may be possible to restrict access to the cell phone in the evenings once the parent returns home from work.
10. It may be stressful for you to set an expectation for your child to participate in normal activities when he or she does not feel well. For some parents, this stress and guilt can make it difficult to stay consistent with their reward systems. In Chapter 8 you will learn more about strategies you can use to manage stress related to caring for your child.

Different Reward Systems for Different Families

Here are a few examples of how other parents of children with chronic pain have used reward systems, and how their children responded when their parents discussed the plans with them.

- "Our plan was for my daughter to attend 1 hour of school four times during the week. Each week we would increase this by 1 hour. She wasn't happy about losing privileges if she didn't attend school, but she liked the reward part."
  —*Susan, mother of a 15-year-old with neck and shoulder pain*

- "We chose to reward two things that we thought she'd be successful with—socializing with friends and getting to

volunteer work. She responded positively and accepting, and added her own suggestions."
—*Betsy, mother of a 13-year-old with foot and leg pain*

- "The privilege system, instead of points, worked better for Elsa. She has even been asking me what she could help me with! She did not do this before, even when she was feeling better."
—*Nancy, mother of a 16-year-old with fibromyalgia*

- "I chose to reward yard work, summer reading for school, and football practice participation. My son seemed to like having a goal and something he really wanted at the end."
—*Mary, mother of a 15-year-old with chronic migraines*

Implementing Praise, Attention, and Reward Systems Can Be Challenging!

You may already give your child praise and attention for coping positively with pain. You may think that praising your child even more is not likely to change his or her behavior. You are partly correct. Increasing praise and attention for positive coping will not change your child's behaviors and response to pain right away. Instead, you can expect a gradual improvement in your child's behaviors over time. It may take a few months before you notice a difference.

Parents who use praise, attention, and reward systems to reinforce positive coping behaviors have children who have less pain and greater ability to participate in important activities.

If you consistently give extra praise and attention over the next few months, your child will learn that you value his or her efforts to cope with pain. Your child will also learn that you believe that he or she can get better at managing pain. Over time, you will see an increase in positive coping behaviors. You can also see a decrease in the level of pain and an increase in your child's participation in important activities.

It can be very challenging to change how you respond to your child's pain. It may seem cold or uncaring to not attend to every complaint of pain. There are many other ways you can show care and concern for your child. For example, you can praise your child for using positive coping behaviors when he or she is in pain. You can also offer to spend special time with your child when he or she shows positive coping behaviors. Making these changes may be difficult, but they are in your child's best interest in the long term. In our experience, parents who use praise, attention, and reward systems to reinforce positive coping behaviors have children who have less pain and greater ability to participate in valued activities.

Reward Systems Encourage Independence

One reason that reward systems are so valuable is that they can help your child become more independent over time. This is especially relevant for older children and adolescents over the age of 10. You can support your teen's independence by allowing him or her to make his or her own mistakes without you always coming to the rescue. For instance, if your child chooses not to attend school and you know this will mean he or she won't have enough points for a new video game, don't feel like you have to help your child go to school. Your child knows the system and will learn from mistakes as well as from successes. You will learn more about how to support your teen's growing independence in Chapter 9.

Involving Others

If other adults spend a significant amount of time with your child, talk with them about the types of behaviors you are trying to praise and reward.

Family Members

Explain to other adult family members what your expectations are for your child and ask their assistance in communicating the same expectations when they spend time with your son or daughter. Ask indulgent grandparents not to give your child rewards or privileges he or she hasn't earned. Parents who are divorced or separated should try to maintain the same strategies for using praise, attention, and reward systems.

School Personnel

You have been learning about making changes that will increase your child's success in achieving important goals, like school attendance. It is useful also to consider how consistency in expectations can be maintained at school. One way to increase consistency at school is to make sure teachers and administrators understand that you want your son or daughter to be in school as much as possible and that you do not want him or her to be sent home each time your child complains of pain. You can also request that your child be permitted to practice relaxation strategies in the classroom or in another location (such as the health room or nurse's office). In Chapter 7 you will learn about additional strategies for working with school staff to increase your child's success at school.

Summary

This chapter introduced the principles for changing problematic child behavior:

- Behaviors followed by positive outcomes are strengthened.
- Behaviors followed by negative outcomes are weakened.

We reviewed how to use attention and praise to increase your child's positive coping behaviors, and we provided instructions for developing and using reward systems to help your child participate in important activities. While implementing a reward system may be challenging at first, consistent use of the plan communicates to your child that positive coping behaviors and increased activity participation are important goals for him or her. As your child masters the initial goals you set, you can revisit the plan together to develop new goals.

Chapter 4   Practice Assignment

You can practice using attention by increasing the amount of verbal praise you give your child when he or she is doing something positive to cope with pain. You can also make a reward system to increase your child's participation in important activities. Decide on either a privilege or a point system and put the expectations and rewards in place. Use the worksheets in Appendices E and F to make a reward system and share it with your child. Communicate the system and rewards with other relevant adults to ensure consistency in how the system is implemented.

List the behaviors or activities that you want to work on in a reward system. Remember that these are the behaviors and activities that you'd like to see your child do more frequently.

1. _____

2. _____

3. _____

4. _____

5. _____

Lifestyle Factors

Samantha was a level 8 gymnast who practiced 16 hours a week. Because of her pain, she has not been able to practice gymnastics lately at all. It has been difficult for her to do any vigorous physical activity. She misses her friends from gymnastics and is worried that if she ever does get to return to practice she will be very behind.

THE GOAL OF THIS CHAPTER IS FOR YOU TO LEARN HOW LIFESTYLE factors affect pain. Lifestyle factors include aspects of daily life such as physical activity, diet, and nutrition that relate to overall health and well-being. Many children experience a decline in the quality of their lifestyles because of their pain problems. They may stop playing sports, become more sedentary (less active), or gain weight. We will review several strategies for supporting positive changes in your child's lifestyle. These strategies will focus on making small changes that add up over time to large benefits.

Pain and Lifestyle

Lifestyle factors are important for all people with chronic pain, including children. Chronic pain may disrupt certain aspects of your child's lifestyle and may lead to unhealthy habits. These poor lifestyle habits may in turn lead to weakening of the muscles and weight gain, and they may increase physical stress on the body, which can result in more pain.

Most parents of children with chronic pain notice a number of concerning differences in their children's lifestyles. "Now, my child is very inactive," says Rita, the mother of a 12-year-old with chronic musculoskeletal pain. "He started gaining excess weight from around 10 years old, and overeating has been a challenge forever. The obesity is intensifying. It seems to be getting more difficult for him to follow through on plans for physical and social activity."

Physical Activity

Most children are physically active while they carry out their usual daily routines. During elementary school children are very active—running, jumping, and climbing in their everyday play. However, from early adolescence to adulthood there is a dramatic natural decline in physical-activity levels. This is due in part to the increase in sedentary time spent at school and in jobs. It is also due to a change in how free time is spent as children get older (e.g., excessive time spent sitting at the computer, watching television, or playing video games). In fact, recent surveys conducted by the Centers for Disease Control and Prevention (CDC) in the United States show that only 18% of children and adolescents meet national guidelines for recommended physical activity. These guidelines suggest that children participate in an activity that increases their heart rate and makes them breathe hard some of the time for at least 60 minutes per day. Because many schools no longer offer physical education classes to students, it is even more challenging for children to obtain vigorous activity during the day. Girls are also less likely than boys to get adequate physical activity, especially later in adolescence. Thus, as a parent, it is easy to see how getting the right amount of physical activity can be a problem for children.

Physical activity and chronic pain are related in a few ways. Studies have shown that more nonactive time makes children more likely to develop chronic pain. In particular, excessive sitting (often to engage in computer and electronic activities) is related to children being more likely to develop neck and back pain in the future. Then, once children have chronic pain, studies show that children's physical activity levels often decrease as a result of activities becoming more difficult to perform. Children spend more time being sedentary (sitting still), and they become deconditioned and lose strength in their muscles. Weak muscles can contribute to worse pain, making it even harder to participate in physical activities like sports or even normal daily activities like walking around school, dressing, or bathing.

"This chronic pain that she has had for 2 years has stopped her from exploring sports at high school. She also could not participate in PE, so she did not get to learn how to exercise to keep her body healthy."
—Tasha, mother of a 16-year-old with chronic migraines

Children may also become fearful of physical activity because of their pain problems. Kids commonly avoid those activities that they think might lead to more pain, or they may worry about injury. These children may choose to only participate in activities they feel are safe, which are most often sedentary activities. Lastly, when children have previously had a high level of competence in a sport or activity, it can be frustrating to participate at a less advanced level on account of the pain problem.

How Do I Know If It Is Safe for My Child to Be Physically Active?

If you have questions about whether it is safe for your child to engage in physical activity, consult with your child's healthcare team. It is important to know whether or not the health professionals who care for your child have placed any restrictions on his or her physical activities. Some restrictions may have been suggested early on while your child's pain problem was being evaluated. However, it is very uncommon for activity restrictions to be placed on children long term. Ask your child's doctors directly whether it is safe for your child to exercise. Your doctor may be able to give advice on appropriate expectations to set for your child's physical activity. A conversation about this issue will put your mind at ease if you have concerns or if you have heard conflicting advice from different sources. This conversation will also enable you to more effectively support your child's efforts to be more physically active.

Five Strategies for Supporting Physical Activity

We recommend that you learn about and make use of five strategies for supporting your child to be physically active:

1. *Support exercise interventions, physical therapy, and occupational therapy.* For children who have been referred for physical therapy or for any form of exercise intervention, parents can use behavioral strategies to reinforce the recommendations made.
2. *Increase the ratio of uptime vs. downtime*—that is, focus on ways to encourage your child to be active instead of inactive.
3. *Schedule pleasant activities* that require your child to be active.
4. *Encourage activity pacing*; this refers to how your child can gradually increase the amount of time that he or she engages in a physical activity before resting.
5. *Use positive language* to set appropriate expectations and reduce fears about pain and injury.

As you learn about each of these strategies, keep in mind that small changes are important to start with. It can feel overwhelming to focus on making too many changes at once. Fortunately, small changes can lead to a series of successes in increasing physical activity.

EXERCISE INTERVENTIONS, PHYSICAL THERAPY, AND OCCUPATIONAL THERAPY

Exercise interventions such as those used in physical therapy (PT) and occupational therapy (OT) may have been recommended for treatment of your child's chronic pain. PT is especially recommended for children with muscle or joint pain (e.g., back pain, hip pain) and for children with complex regional pain syndrome (CRPS). OT is typically recommended for children who have difficulty completing activities of daily living (e.g., dressing, bathing, writing, sitting at a desk) and for children who have pain from non-painful stimuli such as light touch, clothing, bedsheets, or water spray from the shower. When children work with physical therapists, the treatment program may include therapeutic exercise such as a walking or strengthening program, which is aimed at improving aerobic capacity and weight-bearing and functional activities. Therapists may also address general fitness level or restricted range of motion. In addition, specific PT treatments may be used, such as electrical stimulation, massage, or heat, to relieve pain or stiffness. When children work with occupational therapists, the treatment program may include specific exercises to strengthen muscles needed to complete activities of daily living (e.g., hand and arm strength), as well as desensitization exercises (e.g., applying towel rubs to body parts that are sensitive to touch). PT and OT may include training in the use of assistive mobility devices (e.g., wheelchairs), but more often this training will focus on how to walk without the use of these devices. Children who work with physical and occupational therapists will most typically be assigned a home exercise plan as part of the treatment.

> A reward plan can help your child participate in PT and OT visits and complete his or her PT/OT home exercise assignments.

You can develop a reward plan to help your child participate in PT and OT visits and complete his or her home exercise plan. If your child is working with a physical or occupational therapist, be sure you understand exactly what home exercise program has been recommended. For example, if the therapist has recommended a program of 15 minutes of walking each day, then this specific activity can be added to a reward plan and paired with reinforcement or rewards. See Chapter 4 for a review of how to develop a reward plan.

UPTIME VS. DOWNTIME

Even if your child is not presently participating in PT or OT, you can focus on an overall increase in physical activity level (and fitness) in a reward plan. It can be useful to divide activities into downtime, such as sitting or lying down, and uptime, meaning activities that require standing, walking, and moving one's legs. The goal for children who have some limitations in their endurance or tolerance for physical activities is to increase uptime.

Increased ability to carry out regular activities that involve standing and walking can help improve participation in school and social

activities. It can also help with completion of chores and responsibilities. Regular uptime during the day can also help improve sleep,
because physical activity during the day can prepare our bodies to
rest at night. Regular uptime can gradually improve muscle tone,
conditioning, and strength, while downtime can lead to reduction in
fitness and to muscle weakening. Weak muscles can lead to increased
sensations of muscular pain. Therefore, a straightforward goal is to
have your child engage in as much uptime as possible.

Many children with chronic pain do not feel like they are able to
participate in regular activity. Your child may experience an increase
in pain when he or she performs certain activities. Your child may
feel like he or she does not have much energy, so physical activity
may need to be increased gradually.

You can make progress toward the goal of increasing your child's
overall physical activity level by targeting uptime. At the most basic
level, this means getting your child up and moving during the day
and spending less time sitting. For example, together you and your
child can find ways for him or her to stay upright during the day
through doing simple daily tasks. Try asking your child to accomplish a given task in the living room instead of in the bedroom, to
prevent him or her from staying in bed to finish the task. Ask your
child to get the mail, help with dinner preparation, or to feed pets;
these activities will get your child up and moving but are not too
strenuous. At the same time, limits can be set on specific sedentary
activities, especially screen time (e.g., 60-minute limit on television
or computer time) to reduce overall sedentary activity.

A Note About Screen Time

Sometimes the increased difficulty of physical activities for
children with pain can lead to an increase in time spent in
front of screens (e.g., cell phones, iPads, laptops, television).
We have seen this happen even in families that have always
had strict rules about limiting screen time in the family. As
the mother of 13-year-old James told us, "Playing video games
is the only time he doesn't complain of pain." So it can be hard

as a parent to limit an activity that is associated with comfort in light of so few other things bringing comfort to children with chronic pain. However, this time spent in front of screens takes time away from other more physically active options. Taken to the extreme, it can consume large portions of children's waking hours. This is especially true when children are spending more time in the home and not attending school. In this case, James began to spend 7–8 hours a day playing video games. A major focus of his pain treatment for his chronic migraines involved setting limits on video games and expecting regular uptime.

What else can you do as a parent to help your child or teen engage in more regular uptime? As mentioned, an important strategy is to set limits on screen time, which serves to limit downtime. Verbally praise your child for being up on his or her feet and moving, or make it one of the target activities on a reward chart. You can also provide gentle suggestions and help your child understand that excessive downtime is not helpful for the pain problem. You can model good habits of physical activity yourself, and limit your own screen time. If your child sees you engaging in fun physical activities, he or she will be more likely to want to do similar activities. See Chapter 8 for more information on modeling positive behaviors. You can also work with your child to help him or her access opportunities to be active regularly, such as local recreation classes. Some children enjoy physical activities more if a friend is invited to join in the activity. Prompts can also be effective, such as asking your child to join you on a walk or to come to the gym with you. Also try to find physical activities that the whole family can enjoy doing together, such as a family walk, hike, or bike ride.

Model good habits of physical activity yourself, and limit your own screen time.

How you talk about physical activity is also important. You may learn that your son or daughter responds negatively to requests to "go for a walk" because he or she views exercise as unpleasant. But the same child may find a request to go shopping, which involves the same amount of walking, to be much more enticing.

SCHEDULING PLEASANT ACTIVITIES

Many physical activities are those we expect children to perform because they "have to" or "need to." These can include attending school or completing chores. But these activities may feel very difficult to accomplish when in pain and may not be very enjoyable to your child. Many children with chronic pain have to work even harder at school and elsewhere because they have less energy, are fatigued, or are behind in their studies from missing school.

You may feel conflicted about focusing on time for your child to do fun activities if he or she is not performing the essential ones, but fun activities can be an important strategy to help increase your child's physical activity level. First, fun activities are usually met with less resistance than are required activities. Second, fun activities may provide a distraction that helps your child to be physically active for longer periods of time than for required activities. This can help build stamina and endurance for performing other essential activities later. Third, fun activities can lift your child's mood, which may encourage him or her to meet other goals.

The strategy is fairly easy. You can either use our premade list of fun activities or generate your own. It is important to have a broad range of activities on the list (e.g., visiting places of interest, dancing, going to the library). They should all be possible on any given day and should not involve a financial cost that is unfeasible for your family.

For young children (under 10 years old), parents play a major role in the child's activity participation because children this age rely on their parents to select and schedule the activities and to transport them to and from activities. In Chapter 9, you will learn more about supporting young children in being physically active and choosing pleasant activities.

Some pleasant activities you might suggest to your child include the following:

- Shopping or window shopping
- Going to the library or bookstore

- Going for a walk at a park
- Going to the movies
- Shopping for a magazine at the store
- Taking photos or making a video
- Dancing
- Making crafts
- Cooking or baking
- Watching a live sporting event
- Playing with pets

Note that these suggestions range in the intensity of physical activity required, but they all serve the purpose of getting your child moving. Ask your child to look through the list or to come up with his or her own activities. Next, set a specific goal for each week, such as participating in three activities. If you are using a reward system with your child, you can add participation in pleasant activities. If you are not using a reward system, you can chart these activities on a calendar.

"Ellie's biggest fear when she's not having pain is worrying about what can trigger it and being careful to avoid the activity," says Grace, the mother of a 14-year-old with back pain. "It affects her daily because we have not pinpointed what triggers it." As mentioned, some children worry that participating in activities is going to make the pain worse or lead to injury or re-injury. Ideally, once your child begins to participate in more physical activity and sees that the pain doesn't get worse, his or her fears will start to go away. It can also be helpful to start with a very low-intensity physical activity, and gradually increase the intensity and duration of the activity over time. As discussed in Chapter 4, when you are trying to help your child change a behavior, we recommend starting with goals that he or she is very likely to achieve so that the child experiences success early on. But it can sometimes be hard for parents to figure out the balance between pushing and encouraging their child to do more but also listening to the child's fears when he or she tries to do physical activities. *Activity pacing* and *positive language* can be especially helpful for children who are fearful of pain with activity.

> Ideally, once your child begins to participate in more physical activity and sees that the pain doesn't get worse, his or her fears will start to go away.

ACTIVITY PACING

Activity pacing is a method whereby a person structures activities in a way that will prevent overdoing it and worsening pain. Using time (rather than the completion of the activity) as a measure is most common; a person will take rest periods after a certain amount of active time has passed. For example, Anne, who has fibromyalgia, wants to clean her home, but cleaning for several hours almost always increases her pain so much that she is in bed for most of the next day. By learning how to use activity pacing, Anne can clean without making her pain worse. The goal with pacing is for the individual to use time to pace activities, which is important because it enables the person to succeed with a given task without an increase in pain. Anne may clean for 10 minutes, then rest for 5 minutes, clean for 10 minutes, then rest for 5 minutes, and so on. Alternating activity and rest periods may prevent overdoing the activity and worsening pain.

How One Teen Used Activity Pacing to Participate in an Important Social Gathering

Hannah is a 16-year-old girl who has chronic back pain. She gets easily fatigued when she is standing for long periods of time, and standing makes her back pain worse. Hannah's friends like to ice skate. Typically, a small group of her friends skate together for 1 to 2 hours. Hannah finds that when she skates with her friends she ends up spending the rest of the weekend lying in bed to recover from the significant increase in back pain. Then Hannah learned about activity pacing and how it might allow her to skate with her friends without leading to overwhelming pain. Hannah felt that she could skate for about 15 minutes before noticing a significant increase in pain. Her initial goal was to use this starting point for the activity but to add a rest period. Hannah came up with the idea of asking a friend to get a snack and to sit with her during a rest period of 15 minutes. She tried this pattern of 15 minutes skating and 15 minutes sitting, and alternating for the duration of the time at the ice skating rink. She set a timer on her cell phone to remind her when it was time to switch. Hannah was very successful using this technique. The next week she increased her skating time to 20 minutes, without having a significant increase in pain.

POSITIVE LANGUAGE

Your child may have his or her own thoughts and fears about whether performing certain activities will increase pain. You may have heard your child say things like "I don't want to play volleyball today because I know it's going to make my pain worse." You may have your own worries that your child's pain may increase with certain activities. Maybe you keep them to yourself, or maybe you express them to your child directly ("you're right—you should probably stay home from practice today)" or indirectly (e.g., by not reminding your child about volleyball practice because you don't think she'll be able to do it). Because your child will look to you for guidance about how to handle all of the many challenges in daily life, it is very important that you set appropriate expectations and use language that expresses confidence in his or her ability to accomplish difficult things.

Think about how you can support your child's participation in feared activities, by setting the expectation that he or she will participate and persevere (e.g., "I know you will be able to finish your homework after you take a break"). Resist the urge to let your child give up when activities become difficult. The language that you use to talk about your child's abilities should be positive and encouraging (e.g., "you are getting stronger and your body is able to do many things now"). Relaxation and self-calming statements can also be used to stay calm while working to increase time in activities.

Weight, Diet, and Nutrition

Weight issues are important for many children with chronic pain. Some children and adolescents with chronic pain were overweight or obese before their pain problems started; others may experience an increase in weight because of their pain and now be at risk for obesity. As mentioned earlier, having chronic pain may make it harder for children to be physically active, and this inactivity can contribute to additional weight gain. Obesity may need specific treatment through nutrition and diet counseling or with an intensive behavioral intervention program at a specialized pediatric obesity clinic. If you feel that your child would benefit from treatment specifically to help with weight, talk with your child's physician about options in your community.

You can address weight issues at home in part by focusing on improving your child's diet and nutrition, and by supporting him or her to do the same. For some pain conditions, diet and nutrition have likely already been discussed during previous medical evaluations. For example, specific dietary recommendations may be made for a child with suspected celiac disease and abdominal pain (i.e., gluten-free diet) or for a child with migraine headaches (e.g., to avoid foods containing monosodium glutamate). In addition, some studies have shown that increasing overall fluid intake may be helpful in the management of chronic daily headache. Therefore, if your child has headaches or abdominal pain you may have already talked with your child's health providers about how diet and nutrition may relate to the pain problem. In addition, if your child is very overweight and has musculoskeletal pain, you may have had a conversation with your child's pediatrician about the potential benefits of weight loss for your child's pain problem.

> If you feel that your child would benefit from treatment specifically to help with weight, talk with your child's physician about options in your community.

There are many available resources that provide basic nutritional information to support healthy weight loss. Your child's pediatrician is one professional resource who can review weight management with you and your child. While it is beyond the scope of this book to review weight management strategies, we will discuss here two specific issues that seem to more commonly impact children with chronic pain: the regularity of meals and drinking fluids.

Regularity of Meals

The regularity of meals is an important part of every child's lifestyle because it affects overall body health and well-being. Our bodies function best when we eat well and at regular times. For example, for children who do not eat regular meals, going too many hours without food may lead to changes in blood sugar, dizziness, low energy, and tension headaches. We have also seen children with abdominal pain who do not like the sensation of fullness after eating because any increased sensation in their abdomen makes them think that pain will worsen. These children may skip meals but then feel worse the next time they eat because the physical sensations in their abdomen become stronger. Skipping meals may also interfere with physical-activity goals because this leads to low energy levels.

Several strategies can be used to help children and adolescents improve regularity of meals. First, it is important to communicate an expectation that meals will occur at regular times of the day. Even if your child has an irregular schedule because he or she is not attending school, regular meal times can be established. Second, you can continue to serve a range of healthy nutritious foods even if your child has altered his or her diet. We have had patients who significantly altered their diet because of their pain problem; for example, one young girl would only eat soft foods after experiencing severe throat and jaw pain. An important part of her treatment plan was to expose her to a range of healthy foods at regular meals so that she could work toward re-establishing a healthy diet.

Drinking Fluids

Regularity of fluids is also an important eating habit for children with chronic pain. Children with pain need access to liquids throughout the day. If your child has chronic headaches and you want him or her to try drinking more fluids, educate your child about quantity and type of fluids (e.g., limiting caffeinated drinks). In studies that have shown benefit from fluid intake for headache, large amounts of liquid were consumed (1–3 liters a day is recommended). The only way to accomplish this is to drink regularly throughout the day. Most children know what a 2-liter soda bottle looks like; you can talk about this as a goal for the amount of fluid to drink. We suggest that children carry a water bottle to school and on outings and to fill it at least twice to make sure they are getting enough to drink. You can provide rewards for your child reaching fluid-related goals, such as having an empty water bottle at the end of an outing. You may need to talk to your child's school staff to get permission for your child to have a water bottle with him or her in the classroom. You will learn more about working with school staff in Chapter 7.

Because what we drink matters as much as the amount we drink, it is important for your child to be aware of how much caffeine is

We suggest limiting
overall intake
of caffeine and
avoiding it after
lunch to make sure
it doesn't interfere
with falling asleep
at bedtime.

present in the beverages that he or she enjoys. Caffeine is the most popular drug in the world. Caffeine can temporarily make us feel more alert by blocking sleep-inducing chemicals in the brain, and many people use it to feel alert during the day. Caffeine is present in many beverages and foods, including coffee, tea, sodas, and chocolate. There are two specific problems with caffeine. First, caffeine is a diuretic, meaning that it makes the body lose fluid. This works against the goal of increasing fluids in the body. Second, because caffeine can make people alert, having caffeinated foods or drinks in the evening can interfere with falling asleep at night. As you will learn in Chapter 6, difficulties with falling asleep and staying asleep are common for many children with chronic pain.

A general rule of thumb about caffeine is that overall intake should be limited and it should be avoided after lunch to make sure it doesn't interfere with falling asleep at bedtime. As a parent, you can monitor and limit availability of caffeinated beverages in your home and offer decaffeinated beverages in the evening hours. You may need to take your child shopping to make new beverage choices if he or she has previously preferred caffeinated drinks or has a limited range of preferences.

Tips for Addressing Health Habits

In general, it is a fair assumption that children do not want to hear a lecture about the benefits of healthy diet and nutrition. But there are ways you can help your child to understand that health habits are important for pain management. Here are some small changes you can make to help your child and family improve their eating habits. Remember that small changes add up to large benefits over time.

- Have regularly scheduled family meal times as often as is feasible during the week, and reduce reliance on fast-food meals.
- Provide healthy food and drink choices for all meals and snacks.

- Ask children to grocery shop with you so that they can choose new things to try.
- Involve your child in meal preparation. After helping to prepare a healthy meal, your child may be much more likely to try new foods.
- Praise positive eating choices.
- Encourage eating of fruits, vegetables, and high-fiber foods, such as whole-grain breads and cereals, by offering them at meals.
- Support your child in reducing caffeine intake by not buying caffeinated soda pop and by serving milk or water with meals.
- Demonstrate your own healthy habits by making nutritious food choices, limiting screen time, and being physically active.

Summary

In this chapter, we reviewed the importance of lifestyle factors for children with chronic pain. We summarized the negative impact that pain problems may have on physical activity, weight, and nutrition. We reviewed five strategies for increasing physical activity, as well as methods of supporting positive lifestyle changes in weight and nutrition. These methods can help empower children to pursue healthy lifestyles and habits, and to incorporate these into their pain management strategies.

Chapter 5   Practice Assignment

Activity, eating, and drinking habits are some of the most difficult habits for people to change. Luckily, small changes can add up to big benefits, especially for children with chronic pain. Don't expect the changes you want to happen overnight. Instead, choose two to three small changes that you believe you can succeed in. Could you go on a family walk after dinner instead of watching TV? Could you invite your child to plan a healthy meal with you? Could you hand your child a full water bottle when he or she leaves for school? Could you model less screen time and more physical activity for your child to see? These small changes can help your child develop healthy lifestyle habits.

List two or three things you could do to help support improvements in your child's lifestyle habits. Remember, these are hard changes to make, and they don't have to happen all at once. Just pick a few things that you want to work on this week.

These are ways that I will work on improving lifestyle habits:

1. _____

_____

2. _____

_____

3. _____

_____

Sleep Interventions

Amber is 17 years old and has chronic jaw and neck pain and migraine headaches. She has been unable to fall asleep until 2 or 3 A.M. each night despite getting into bed around 9 or 10 P.M. Amber is so sleepy in the morning when her alarm goes off to wake her for school that she often cannot get out of bed. When she does make it to school, she falls asleep in class.

THIS CHAPTER WILL REVIEW COMMON SLEEP PROBLEMS EXPERIenced by children with chronic pain. You will learn about normal sleep needs in children, how to promote good sleep habits, and strategies to treat specific sleep problems, such as bedtime resistance and insomnia.

Pain can affect anyone's ability to settle to sleep and stay asleep, and children are no exception. Not sleeping well can have a profound impact on children's ability to cope with pain, their mood, and their participation in daytime activities. For parents and children struggling with sleep issues, it may seem like sleep will improve on its own once the pain problem gets better, but many children continue to struggle with poor sleep even when their pain improves.

Poor sleep in children can also have an impact on parents' sleep. Your child may wake you during the night to ask for help going to sleep or staying asleep. We recommend that sleep intervention be included in every child's pain management plan so that existing sleep problems are addressed and/or to prevent future problems with sleep from developing.

Sleep Problems and Their Impact on Children with Chronic Pain

Not getting enough sleep makes people feel pain more acutely and makes it harder to cope with chronic pain. Studies have shown that not getting enough sleep or good-quality sleep makes pain sensations feel worse the next day. So sleep loss can actually cause more pain.

Common sleep problems experienced by children with chronic pain include the following:

- Difficulties settling to sleep
- Waking frequently during the night
- Not feeling rested
- Not getting an adequate amount of sleep

In addition, children may limit social activities that involve sleep (sleepovers, camp, etc.) for fear of how problems with sleep may interfere.

Children with chronic medical problems tend to have more sleep problems than children without medical problems. These sleep issues may be related to treatments for the medical condition itself (such as medications) or to symptoms that interfere with sleep (inflammation, pain). Children may also develop habits that lead to problems with insomnia symptoms (chronic difficulties with falling asleep or staying asleep).

"Because she is tired all the time it's hard to get her out of her bed. In the morning, I am not sure if is she having problems because she didn't sleep well."

—Patricia, mother of a 15-year-old girl with fibromyalgia

Having sleep problems makes it harder for children to cope with chronic pain because sleep loss affects mood, leading to more negativity and increased irritability. Anxiety and depression are also associated with sleep problems, and sleep may become a source of concern or worry for children, leading to anxiety about falling and staying asleep. Not getting enough sleep can lead to high levels of fatigue and daytime sleepiness, causing many children to lose interest in daytime activities. For some children, the combination of pain and sleep problems makes getting out of bed each morning very difficult. Performance in regular and vigorous physical activities is negatively affected by sleep loss. Sleep can also affect a child's ability to concentrate, complete schoolwork, and perform in athletics and sporting events.

Sleep Needs of Children

It is well understood that important functions that keep us healthy occur during sleep. Everyone progresses through five stages of sleep, ranging from light to deep sleep, during the night. During deep sleep, growth hormone is released in children and young adults, and many of the body's cells show increased production of proteins during deep sleep. Since proteins are the building blocks needed for cell growth and for repair of damage from factors like stress, deep sleep is truly important. In addition, activity in parts of the brain that control emotions, decision-making processes, and social interactions is drastically reduced during deep sleep. Scientists believe that this type of sleep may help people to function better emotionally and socially while they are awake.

How much sleep does a child really need? In large part, the answer to this question depends on the age of the child. Children require a certain amount of sleep to function well, but that amount varies. Children under 10 years of age will need 10–11 hours of sleep, while adolescents will need about 9 hours of sleep per night. Adults, on the other hand, need about 8 hours of sleep.

This may sound like more sleep than you would have thought necessary. Certainly there is a large amount of variability in sleep needs. Some people seem to function well on less than the recommended amount of sleep, while other people seem to need much longer sleep times. Many people are chronically sleep deprived and have learned to get by on minimal sleep. The sleep times quoted here are rough guidelines; the important point is that across development, children's sleep needs shift, and this happens at the same time as other important biological and social changes in childhood.

Polls conducted by the National Sleep Foundation show that the amount of sleep an average high school student gets is much less than the recommended amount, at only 7 to 7½ hours per night (http://www.sleepfoundation.org/). Most teens do not get adequate sleep, for a number of reasons. One is the competing demands of schoolwork, jobs, or social pressures (e.g., responding to text messages) that occur at night and that make it difficult to protect a teenager's sleep time. Another important reason is biology. During puberty, teens experience a shift in their circadian rhythm (or "body clock"), which makes them feel alert during later hours in the evening (making it easier to stay up late) and sleepier in the early morning hours (making it easier to stay in bed). The average teen sleeps in on weekends, sometimes until the afternoon, and this habit may make it difficult to establish a regular sleep schedule.

"Sleep is a major issue. She does not get long stretches of sleep . . . more like 1 1/2 to 2 hours at a stretch."
—Doug, father of a 16-year-old girl with chronic back pain

As young children develop into adolescents, sleep management by parents may change. Bedtimes and bedtime routines that parents were once very involved in may alter into routines that a teenager carries out by him- or herself. Most parents of teens are unaware of what time their teen actually falls asleep at night or how much time their teen actually spends sleeping after he or she goes to bed.

Sleep Habits

Establishing good sleep habits is especially important for children with chronic pain. *Sleep habits* refer to the behaviors, activities, and routines that affect how children settle to sleep, and the regularity of their sleep. Even if children are not currently having serious problems with their sleep, establishing good sleep habits now can help prevent problems from developing in the future. In the next sections we discuss eight tips for good sleep habits:

1. Keep a regular sleep schedule
2. No weekend catch-up sleep
3. Limit naps

4. Pay attention to healthy lifestyle habits
5. Use beds only for sleeping
6. Develop relaxing bedtime routines
7. Minimize electronics in the bedroom and at bedtime
8. Schedule adequate sleep for your child's needs

1. Keep a Regular Sleep Schedule

As mentioned, across childhood there may be changes in how parents monitor their children's sleep and in how bedtimes and sleep schedules are handled. Typically, younger children have a regular bedtime. But, as children get older, the schedule may relax. By the teen years, bedtime may not occur at a particular set time. However, even for teenagers, keeping a sleep schedule is critical, for several reasons. Consistent sleep schedules help ensure that kids get enough sleep and that sleep occurs around the same time each day; both of these factors are important for a healthy sleep routine. Parents can help their child or teen keep a schedule that allows him or her to wake up and go to bed at about the same time every day (even when it is not a school day). This is important because our bodies like regularity: When we go to bed and wake up at regular times, our bodies learn to be sleepy at bedtime and alert at the time we want to wake up.

2. No Weekend Catch-up Sleep

As mentioned earlier, our bodies like regularity, and keeping to a schedule helps with obtaining enough sleep. When left to manage their own schedules, most teens would choose to sleep in on the weekends, sometimes until the afternoon. But if your teen sleeps in late on Saturday and Sunday mornings, it will be harder for him or her to fall asleep at the right time and maintain the proper schedule during the school week.

A general rule of thumb is to not vary waking times by more than 1 to 2 hours from day to day. This means that if your child needs to wake up on school days by 7:00 A.M., then he or she should not sleep beyond 9:00 A.M. on weekends. Preventing weekend catch-up sleep can help keep your child's sleep schedule on track. You will know your child is on a regular schedule when he or she feels sleepy at predictable times each night and can awaken fairly easily in the morning.

Traveling to Another Time Zone . . . Every Weekend

Think about when you have traveled to a different time zone. How does your body feel trying to adjust to bedtime and waking? When you are several hours off of your normal rhythm, it may take a few days to be able to feel sleepy and alert at the proper times. Some teenagers experience this every weekend when they sleep in 3 or 4 hours off from their normal sleep cycle.

3. Limit Naps During the Day

Many children with chronic pain take naps during the day. The purpose of the nap may be to help a child relieve a headache or to rest because he or she is tired from the school day or wasn't able to sleep the night before. Some pain medications may make children feel drowsy during the day and more likely to nap.

The problem with naps during the day is that they can interfere with keeping a regular sleep schedule at night. Napping, especially in the late afternoon, will likely make it harder for your child to feel sleepy at the regular bedtime. In general, we suggest that you try to limit your child's naps during the day. Try not offering a nap as a solution for when your child is in pain. Instead, offer another of the pain management strategies reviewed in this book. (However, if your child is very sleepy or doesn't feel well, you should help him or her limit the nap to 30 to 45 minutes in the late morning or early afternoon.)

If your older teen is unsupervised after school, you may face some challenges in monitoring whether naps are occurring. One strategy that other parents have used is to call the teen each day after school to check in, which helps to prevent naps.

4. Pay Attention to Healthy Lifestyle Habits

As discussed in Chapter 5, lifestyle habits such as regular physical activity, avoiding caffeine, and eating regular meals are important for children with chronic pain. These same lifestyle habits are also important for helping people feel comfortable and ready for sleep. In particular, we recommend that children reduce caffeine intake, and especially to not have caffeine in the late afternoon, as it can interfere with settling to sleep. In addition, regular activity can help children establish routines that promote regular sleep and wake times. Such activities can include going to school each day, participating in scheduled after-school activities, and having a set time to work on homework in the evenings.

> Lifestyle habits such as regular physical activity, avoiding caffeine, and eating regular meals are important for helping children with chronic pain feel comfortable and ready for sleep.

Smoking and nicotine use can also interfere with settling to sleep because they have stimulant qualities. There is also a relationship between smoking and increased pain. We advise teens in our clinic not to smoke. Parents can play an important role as well by not exposing their children to cigarette smoke and by communicating messages that smoking is not allowed. See Chapter 9 for more information on how to talk to your teen about smoking.

5. Beds Are for Sleeping Only

It is a good habit to reserve the bed only for sleeping; children should feel ready to sleep when they enter the bed. This practice helps with falling asleep quickly and staying asleep. We recommend that you help your child find another place to sit to study, read, use the computer, watch television, text and talk on the phone, or do crafts. Finding another place to carry out these other activities will also give your child more uptime (see Chapter 5 for more information about uptime). You can also make sure the bedroom is comfortable for your child in terms of the temperature (not too hot or too cold), amount of light, noise, and comfort of the bed.

6. Develop Relaxing Bedtime Routines

It is easier to settle to sleep when our bodies and minds are prepared for it. Encourage your child to develop a relaxing bedtime routine that he or she can follow each night. It should involve 20–30 minutes of quiet, wind-down activities like reading, looking at a magazine, listening to music, or writing in a journal. Help protect this time by encouraging your child to finish homework earlier in the evening. Let others in the household know that your child needs to get to sleep. If your child shares a room with a sibling or other family member, it will be particularly important to establish ways to protect your child's bedtime. This may require asking others to be quiet after bedtime and to enter the room only when prepared to sleep. It is important for our bodies to relax and slow down enough to allow sleep to come.

7. Minimize Electronics in the Bedroom and at Bedtime

As mentioned earlier, one of the major social pressures faced by older children and teens is communication that occurs over electronic devices. Many children also prefer activities that involve screen time. Having a television, gaming computer, or cell phone turned on can disrupt your child's bedtime and sleep period. Watching television, using the computer, and watching video games are considered energizing or stimulating activities. It is best to help your child develop other calm activities to precede bedtime.

Your child may also feel social pressure to respond to e-mail or text messages that come at late hours. Charging the cell phone outside of the bedroom at night prevents your child from feeling this pressure. We suggest a family plug-in station for everyone's electronic devices in the kitchen or another room. This is one way to get cell phones out of bedrooms. If your child uses the cell phone as an alarm clock, you may need to purchase a separate alarm clock in order to keep the phone out of the bedroom.

> Studies have shown that children with televisions in their bedrooms go to bed later and get poorer quality sleep compared to children who do not have televisions in their bedrooms.

Keeping televisions out of children's bedrooms is also an important strategy for eliminating television-viewing at bedtime (or after bedtime). Studies have shown that children with televisions in their bedrooms go to bed later and get poorer quality sleep compared to children who do not have televisions in their bedrooms. In general, we recommend limiting the number of electronics in your child's bedroom or sleeping area.

8. *Schedule Adequate Sleep for Your Child's Needs*

It is important to help your child develop a schedule that allows for enough sleep. As mentioned earlier, most teens need about 9 hours of sleep to function at their best, and younger children will need slightly more. This may be more than you or your teen thought. In developing a schedule that allows for enough sleep, you can talk with your child about choices that can be made to establish a more ideal sleep schedule.

We usually explain to children that there are two ends of the schedule (bedtime and wake time) that can be altered to get enough sleep. Their job is to help fit in their necessary activities between these hours. For some children, it is fairly easy to find ways to alter either bedtime or wake time to increase sleep duration. For example, how your child gets to school (e.g., transportation options) may greatly influence the morning wake time. In some families, choices such as carpooling instead of taking the bus may be an option for extending a child's sleep. In addition, performing certain activities the night before (e.g., showers, making lunches, getting materials ready for school) can reduce the number of morning tasks so that sleep can be extended in the morning. In general, most children are more receptive to lengthening the morning wake time than they are to making the bedtime earlier, so it is worth discussing creative options for doing this. We encourage you to sit down with your child and outline a specific sleep schedule that will allow for adequate sleep. Putting in writing a proposed bedtime (e.g., 9:30 P.M.) and wake time (e.g., 7:30 A.M.) can help your child see how it might be possible for him or her to get more sleep.

Making the Sleep Schedule Work

Karly is a 15-year-old girl with chronic headaches who has been having a hard time getting enough sleep. Karly needs to wake up at 5:30 A.M. to get ready for school because the bus picks her up at 6:50 A.M. To get herself ready in the morning, Karly needs to shower, apply makeup, and get school materials together. Most mornings, Karly feels very sleepy when her alarm clock goes off. She often has a headache as well.

Karly has been trying to go to bed at 10:00 P.M. on school nights. When her mom sat down with Karly to review her sleep schedule, she wrote down the current bedtime of 10:00 P.M. and her wake time of 5:30 A.M. They computed the amount of sleep that this schedule would allow for, which is 7.5 hours. Karly's mom stated that the goal was to aim for a schedule that would give her 9 hours of sleep, which is the amount that a teenager needs. Karly was not sure how she could get 1.5 hours' more sleep. She told her mom that she couldn't go to bed at 8:30 P.M. because she would have no free time and wouldn't get her homework done. Then, they discussed her morning routine and whether she really needed to get up at 5:30 A.M. Karly said that she is so sleepy in the morning that it takes her a long time to get ready. She was willing to try to move some activities to nighttime, including showering, making a lunch, and getting school materials together. Karly's mom also agreed to take her to school in the morning instead of having her ride the bus so that she could leave the house at 7:15 A.M. instead of 6:50 A.M. Karly and her mom agreed that she would try out a new schedule: she would wake up at 6:30 A.M. and go to sleep at 9:30 P.M.

Specific Sleep Problems

Bedtime problems, such as the child taking a long time to fall asleep, refusing to settle to sleep, and waking during the night, are very common, occurring in 20% to 30% of all children. Unusual sleep behaviors, such as sleepwalking or waking with bad dreams, may also occur during childhood. Other types of sleep behaviors may come to the parent's attention as well: Children may experience repetitive body movements during the night or may get out of bed in a confused state. There are several types of rhythmic movements that may occur during the night, such as movements of the entire body (e.g., rocking back and forth), headbanging, or repeated leg movements. These actions can be alarming.

There are several problems concerning sleep in childhood that should be evaluated by a sleep specialist. One such problem is *sleep-disordered breathing* (also called *sleep apnea*). This is a disorder that involves pauses in breathing during the night. Children with this problem often have very loud snoring and may be heard making gasping or chok- ing sounds during the night. Evaluation of sleep-disordered breathing is done with an overnight sleep study during which children are monitored for their breathing while asleep in a hospital bed. Sleep-disordered breathing is fairly rare in children, but if you have a concern about sleep-disordered breathing you should talk with your child's physician.

> The most common sleep problems that children with chronic pain are likely to have are bedtime resistance and insomnia.

Most children with chronic pain who have problems with settling to sleep and staying asleep have problems that are somewhat easier to solve. These are *behavioral sleep problems*; they are related to behaviors and not to an underlying physiological problem (such as sleep-disordered breathing). The most common diagnoses of behav- ioral sleep problems that children with chronic pain are likely to have are bedtime resistance and insomnia. Next we discuss strategies for managing these two common sleep problems.

Bedtime Resistance

Bedtime resistance refers to the struggles that children have with being ready to go to sleep at bedtime. Children may delay bedtime by making repeated requests to parents (such as for a glass of water or to be tucked in). Children may also ask or demand that their parents stay in their room while they go to sleep. During the night, children may wake and come to their parents' bedroom to sleep with them (co-sleeping).

While parents may expect that young children will demonstrate some difficulties with sleep, these same struggles can also occur in older children. Chronic pain may result in the return of bedtime struggles in an older child. Sometimes even teens become resistant to bedtime and may want their parents present during the night. Bedtime struggles may become very frequent and prolonged and require a lot of parent time and attention at night. Certainly, a night here and there of co-sleeping may not cause any major disruption, but for some children a pattern can develop that becomes a problem and a source of stress for parents who must manage these behaviors during the night.

Several behavioral strategies are effective for reducing bedtime struggles. *Extinction*, also known as *planned parental ignoring*, involves establishing a regular bedtime routine, bedtime, and wake time and avoiding any response to children's resistance (crying, whining, requests) after being put to bed. The parent ignores these behaviors and does not return to comfort the child or get things after bedtime. Often a reward chart is used to encourage the child to earn rewards for staying in bed and going to bed by him- or herself. Extinction can also be modified so that parents are allowed to remain in the child's room but still ignore and avoid any response to the child. For example, the parent may sit in a chair reading quietly but would not interact with the child. Over time, the parent can move the chair farther away from the child's bed until he or she is sitting outside the child's door. Over time, the child would not require the parents' presence as the child gets used to falling asleep alone.

Some parents have experience using these strategies to address bedtime struggles from when their children were toddlers or preschoolers, but the strategies can also be effective with older children. It is important to remember that *behavior* is most commonly the cause of sleep struggles—it is much less common for pain during the night to cause a problem with sleep. However, if increased pain is interfering with sleep, then children can be reminded to use pain management strategies like deep breathing and relaxation. It is important to encourage your child to use pain management strategies that can be implemented without your assistance. You can learn more about how to help your child manage pain independently in Chapter 9.

It is important to remember that behavior is most commonly the cause of sleep struggles— it is much less common for pain during the night to be causing a problem with sleep.

Insomnia

You have probably heard the word *insomnia* before. Insomnia means "no sleep" in Latin, and it is the most common sleep complaint for children and adults. A person has insomnia symptoms if he or she has difficulty falling asleep or staying asleep, wakes up too early and is unable to get back to sleep, doesn't feel well rested in the morning, or feels that poor sleep is causing problems during the day. While everyone experiences insomnia once in a while, *chronic insomnia* occurs most nights of the week and lasts for several months. It may not be obvious whether your child is having a problem with insomnia; you may need to ask your child whether he or she has any difficulties falling or staying asleep.

There are several techniques that can be helpful for children who are experiencing insomnia symptoms. These include sleep restriction, sleep training, and relaxation methods.

SLEEP RESTRICTION

A common reaction to problems with falling asleep and staying asleep is to begin spending more time in bed. Often this happens because the person hopes that being in bed longer will lead to getting more sleep. Children with chronic pain may spend more time in bed simply because they don't feel well. But lying in bed resting and struggling to fall asleep is counterproductive. Rest is not equivalent to sleep. There are no benefits from having more resting time in bed; instead, it may lead to insomnia or make insomnia symptoms worse.

A strategy that we use to address the problem of spending too much time in bed is sleep restriction. Sleep restriction is also useful for managing and preventing insomnia symptoms in children. Sleep restriction involves delaying your child's bedtime until he or she feels sleepy. For children with chronic pain, temporarily delaying bedtime (making it later) can be very helpful as your child works on developing other strategies to help with sleep. Sleep restriction begins with establishing an initial sleep schedule that matches when the person is actually falling asleep. For example, if a child has been going to bed at 9:00 P.M. but not falling asleep until 11:30 P.M., then we would set an initial (starting) sleep schedule with an 11:30 P.M. bedtime. As the child becomes successful at falling asleep quickly, we can gradually move the bedtime back until it is at a time that allows for adequate sleep.

Too Much Time in Bed

Amelia is a 9-year-old girl with abdominal pain who has been having problems falling asleep. Her parents have moved her bedtime to 8:00 P.M. in hopes that having more time available for sleep will lead to more sleep. Unfortunately, Amelia tosses and turns for several hours. Most often, she gets out of bed around 10:00 P.M. to tell her parents that she can't fall asleep. They give her a few suggestions (such as reading), bring her water, and tuck her back into bed. Eventually, Amelia does fall asleep, around 11:00 P.M.

Sleep restriction was an important strategy used with Amelia and her parents to reduce her struggles to fall asleep. Amelia was asked to start with a temporary bedtime of 11:00 P.M. This seemed very late to Amelia and her parents. We reviewed what activities she was allowed to perform until this bedtime and where they needed to occur (outside the bedroom). This required some family problem-solving. Amelia's 12-year-old sister had a 9:30 P.M. bedtime, and so a family meeting was necessary to avoid conflict over Amelia staying up later than her older sister. The idea of a temporary bedtime that shifts every few days was described in detail so that everyone understood how the sleep restriction was expected to work.

Amelia had good success with this strategy and fell asleep quickly the first few nights at around 11:00 P.M. She moved her bedtime back to 10:45 P.M. for the next few nights and also fell asleep quickly. Amelia and her parents continued to work on good sleep habits during this time. After 2 weeks, Amelia was falling asleep at 9:30 P.M. Because her goal was to obtain about 10 hours of sleep each night, her parents realized that 9:30 P.M. could serve as a final bedtime since her wake time was not until 7:30 A.M. Notice that this was a very different bedtime than where they started.

SLEEP TRAINING

Sleep training (also called *stimulus control*) is a strategy that can be helpful for people who have a hard time falling asleep when they first get into bed, and for people who have a hard time falling back to sleep when they wake up in the night. The goal is to help your child learn to strengthen the connection between getting into bed and feeling ready to sleep. Here we provide the same instructions for sleep training at home that we give to children we see in our clinics.

1. Don't go to bed until you feel sleepy. Note: it is okay if this is quite late. This is a *temporary* bedtime.
2. If you cannot fall asleep within about 20 minutes, get out of bed and do a quiet activity. Note: don't watch the clock, 20 minutes is what it feels like to you. The activities you do should be boring and quiet and do not need to be finished (for example, homework would *not* be a good option).
3. Return to bed when you feel sleepy.
4. Repeat Steps 2 and 3 as often as necessary throughout the night.
5. Use your bed only for sleep (don't read, watch TV, or play games while in bed).
6. Avoid napping during the daytime.
7. Use an alarm clock to wake up at the same time each morning.

We often suggest to children that they set up a "nesting area" to use for sleep training. This can be any place outside of the bed that is ready for your child to go to when he or she can't fall asleep within 20 minutes. It should be made to be appealing to your child, with placement of blankets and reading material or another quiet activity that your child chooses. The goal is for your child to go there and participate in a boring, quiet activity if he or she can't sleep. Then the child should return to bed when he or she is very sleepy. If your child has problems with waking in the middle of the night, try using these same instructions. Your child should get out of bed if he or she is unable to fall back to sleep within 20 minutes and then continue with the same steps.

The Nesting Place: Do's and Don'ts

Here are things that are okay to do in the nesting place: re-read an old book, draw, write a story, do a craft (e.g., knit), use relaxation skills, listen to soft music.

Here are things that are not okay to do in the nesting place: watch TV or videos, clean, use the Internet, get homework done, play video games, use a cell phone.

It takes a few weeks for sleep training to kick in and for children to learn to settle to sleep quickly when entering the bed. In the beginning, bedtimes are made around the time that your child is actually falling asleep, even if this is quite late. Then, gradually, as your child makes progress in falling asleep quickly, bedtimes can be made a little earlier (by 15–30 minutes) until the ideal bedtime is reached. Depending upon how late your child is falling asleep this may take some time. However, sleep training is very effective when the instructions are closely followed, and your child should make good progress in learning to settle to sleep quickly. If your child is not making progress, you should talk with your child's doctor or psychologist about getting additional assistance in implementing treatment for insomnia.

> "I encouraged a calmer bed atmosphere before bedtime. Finishing homework earlier and ending video games and computer time at least an hour before bed was really helpful."
>
> —Joyce, mother of a 14-year-old boy with chronic musculoskeletal pain

RELAXATION STRATEGIES

Another technique that can be useful for falling asleep more quickly is to use deep breathing, relaxation, or imagery strategies at bedtime. "Kate worked on her bedtime routine by listening to the relaxation music and leaving her computer off," said Paula, mother of a 12-year-old girl with chronic abdominal pain. Relaxation can help overcome worries about not falling asleep and can help your child feel more at ease at bedtime. Relaxation can also make your child's muscles less tense and help relieve pain that is present before falling sleep. In Chapter 3, we reviewed relaxation techniques, and these same strategies can be used at bedtime for difficulties with falling asleep. When children are using relaxation to help with sleep, we ask them to practice the same instructions but to start them when they get into the bed to settle to sleep. If children have problems with waking in the middle of the night or waking too early in the morning, they can also use relaxation strategies to settle back to sleep.

Implementing the Sleep Plan Away from Home

Once children accomplish the goal of learning a few techniques to help them fall asleep more easily, they can work on sleep in settings away from home. Here is an example of how a teenage girl with chronic pain implemented her sleep plan away from home.

"Isabella has not spent a night at a friend's house for over a year because of problems with sleep and pain. She has never felt like her friends would truly understand. She overheard a couple girls talking, saying they thought she was faking the insomnia and pain just because she was afraid to spend the night. Isabella took a major step and talked to her two best friends, who were determined they would stick with her all night. She explained how she felt and what her pain was like. She told them she had learned relaxation strategies to help her fall asleep. They really listened and she did it. I couldn't tell you what a mental and physical accomplishment this was. I could not stop telling her how proud we were. Isabella was very proud of herself."

—*Judy, mother of 14-year-old Isabella, who has complex regional pain syndrome (CRPS)*

Medications and Sleep

Because many children with chronic pain take over-the-counter and prescription medications for pain, it is important to consider how medications affect sleep. For example, opioid pain medications affect sleep stages and may interrupt children's ability to achieve deep sleep. Other medications may seem helpful initially for sleep problems because they make children feel tired—for instance, some parents give their children over-the-counter medicines such as anti-histamines to help them feel sleepy. There are also some prescription medicines or supplements that your physician may have prescribed to help your child settle to sleep.

Melatonin is a commonly used over-the-counter sleep aide. This is a natural hormone that is produced by the body and involved in the sleep–wake circadian cycle. Because it is not a regulated medication, there may be differences between brands in the formulation of melatonin. We encourage parents to talk with their child's primary care physician about using melatonin if this is something they have tried or would like to try. Some children seem to benefit.

In general, medicines that have sleepiness as a side effect may be useful in the short term. Unfortunately, all medicines carry a risk of more serious side effects, and medicines won't produce the changes in habits that will improve sleep in the long term. If your child continues to experience problems with his or her sleep even after establishing good sleep habits, you may want to discuss other options for treatment with your child's physician.

> All medicines carry a risk of more serious side effects, and medicines won't produce the changes in habits that will improve sleep in the long term.

If your child is already taking medicines for sleep, it is still very important to work on improving sleep habits and behaviors so that long-term improvements in sleep can be achieved. A goal may be for your child to be weaned off of these medicines, and you can discuss a weaning schedule with your child's physician(s). Having good sleep habits in place will make it easier for your child to achieve this goal.

Parents' Sleep Habits

Although we have focused on how these sleep strategies can benefit your child, the same sleep interventions can also benefit adult sleep.

If you are struggling with your own sleep habits or are having problems falling asleep or staying asleep, we encourage you to try these strategies for yourself. As mentioned in Chapter 1, when parents engage in self-care, their children ultimately benefit. Parents who get good-quality sleep are better prepared to manage the challenges of parenting their children with chronic pain.

Summary

In this chapter, we reviewed the importance of sleep for your child's physical, mental, and social functioning. Sleep is an aspect of daily life that can be easily disrupted by pain and by poor habits that may arise from having alterations in one's schedule (such as not attending school regularly). Fortunately, there are several helpful strategies that can improve sleep habits and lead to a more regular sleep schedule that allows for an age-appropriate amount of sleep. In addition, for children who are struggling with problems falling asleep or staying asleep, sleep training and relaxation strategies may help them learn to settle to sleep more quickly and easily. As a parent, you can protect your child's sleep time, promote good sleep habits, and help encourage use of effective behavioral strategies for difficulties with falling asleep. You can also use some of the same strategies to help improve your own sleep habits.

Chapter 6   Practice Assignment

Choose at least three ways that you can help promote good sleep habits for your child or for yourself. You may choose to work on sleep habits, or on instructing your child in specific sleep strategies for reducing insomnia symptoms, or on trying out strategies to reduce bedtime resistance. Keep in mind that it takes several weeks for new habits to develop, so be patient and stick to it so that you can see the progress over time. If you have a reward system for your child, consider adding sleep habits to the plan.

This week, I will work on my sleep or my child's sleep using the following sleep strategies:

- ☐ Sleep habits:
  - ☐ Keep a regular sleep schedule
  - ☐ No weekend catch-up sleep
  - ☐ Limit naps
  - ☐ Pay attention to healthy lifestyle habits
  - ☐ Use beds only for sleeping
  - ☐ Develop relaxing bedtime routines
  - ☐ Minimize electronics in the bedroom and at bedtime
  - ☐ Schedule adequate sleep for my child's needs
- ☐ Too much time in bed:
  - ☐ Sleep restriction
- ☐ Bedtime resistance or co-sleeping:
  - ☐ Extinction
  - ☐ Reward system
- ☐ Insomnia:
  - ☐ Sleep training
  - ☐ Use of relaxation strategies

School and Social Life

Luke has had problems with school attendance since his back pain started 2 years ago. Over the years, he has missed more and more school. He just started his junior year of high school but is repeating a few classes from last year. At this point, he is so worried that he won't graduate with his friends that the worry itself is making it hard for him to get back on track in school.

T HE GOAL OF THIS CHAPTER IS FOR YOU TO LEARN STRATEGIES TO help your child with problems related to school and social life. Research shows that chronic pain can get in the way of school. Pain can also get in the way of your child's ability to stay connected with friends. From this chapter you will learn how pain can impact schooling and peer relationships, how to manage school refusal and school re-entry by making a school plan, how to work with school staff to help your child reach his or her school goals, and how to support your child's friendships.

How Pain Interferes with School

Pain can get in the way of your child's or teen's schooling in many ways. Pain can make it hard for children to get up in the morning to

Children with chronic pain can struggle in any type of school setting. go to school, or children may leave school early because of pain flares. Pain can also affect children's participation in their schoolwork (e.g., making it hard to read or concentrate). For all of these reasons, school can become a very difficult environment for your child. Sometimes parents make other arrangements to try to help with the problems at school. For example, parents may turn to online school, hoping that a more flexible schedule will lead to more success. However, children completing online coursework may continue to have difficulty getting schoolwork done because of pain. In our experience, children with chronic pain can struggle in any type of school setting.

Research shows that children with chronic pain are often absent from school and identify school as stressful. Missed school can negatively impact your child's grades and his or her ability to reach major milestones like high school graduation. Children with chronic pain may miss so much school that they have significant gaps in instruction and require tutoring, or they may need to repeat courses when they return to school. Even when children with chronic pain attend school, pain itself and pain medications can make it hard to concentrate and learn. Children with chronic pain may have difficulties with teachers or peers who do not understand their pain problem.

Pain, missed school, and missed extracurricular activities can also create difficulties for your child in making and keeping friends. School may be a major source of stress for your child, which can cause increased pain, and this can set in motion a cycle that leads to more pain and more difficulties with school and peers. Here are a few other ways that pain can get in the way of your child's school life:

- Pain at night can make it hard to sleep and to get up for school the next day.
- A pain flare in the morning can make it hard to get to school on time.
- A pain flare during the school day may make your child want to go home early.
- A pain flare after school can make it hard to complete homework.
- Your child may worry about pain starting when he or she is in school and how to deal with it.

- Your child may worry about what teachers or friends will think if he or she has to leave class because of pain or when he or she comes back to school after a long absence.
- Your child may have trouble keeping his or her grades up.
- Your child may worry that he or she will not be able to succeed in college or at a university.
- Your child may have trouble concentrating on schoolwork because of pain or because of medication side effects.
- Missing school and not doing homework can lead to a lot of work to catch up on and, in turn, increase stress.
- Missing school can make it hard to fit in with friends.
- Your child may not be able to participate in after-school sports or clubs.

Making a School Plan: Picking a School Goal

A school plan refers to a concrete set of steps intended to help children reach goals related to school. School plans are important no matter what type of school your child attends, and they can help with school refusal and school re-entry.

Involve your child in choosing his or her school goals. This will make it more likely that your child will follow the school plan.

The first step in making a school plan is to choose a school goal. You may have already identified goals related to school in Chapter 2. Next, talk to your child about how pain interferes with school. This can lead to a conversation about your child's own school goals. It is important to involve your child in choosing his or her school goals, because this will make it more likely that your child will follow the school plan.

Most children and teenagers have a high level of stress about school, so this can be an unpopular topic of conversation. For this reason, it is important to use praise and positive attention (see Chapter 4) when you talk about school goals. Try saying, "I appreciate that you are willing to share your school goals with me. I want to figure out how to help you reach these goals." Show that you are listening by taking the time to talk when you have time to truly focus on this issue. In Chapter 9, we will discuss communication strategies you can use to help with this conversation.

You may have your own goals for your child's schooling. Sometimes parents and children have the same goals in mind, but sometimes these are very different. For example, parents may want to see their child go to school every day. However, the child may want to get good grades but is not interested in being in school more often. Such differences in perspective are normal in families but will need to be discussed. We recommend that the first school plan you make include only your child's goals. Over time, it will become easier to expand on these goals. Here are some examples of school goals your child may want to work on:

- Increasing time spent in school
- Returning to full-time school
- Getting to school when in pain
- Staying in school when in pain
- Improving grades
- Completing schoolwork
- Finishing incomplete courses from previous grading periods
- Becoming more involved in school activities (sports, clubs)
- Returning to regular school (if in online school or homeschool)

Your child may want to work on one school goal at a time, or several at the same time. In Chapter 8, you will learn a specific approach to problem-solving that you and your child can also use to identify school goals and to make a plan for how to address them.

What If My Child Is in Online School?

As we have mentioned, a school plan is important no matter what type of school your child or teen attends. Children in online school can face different types of challenges in meeting their school goals:

- Low motivation to work on schoolwork compared to that for other, more desirable activities available at home (napping, playing video games, watching YouTube videos, etc.)
- Trouble keeping up a good pace with schoolwork
- Increased obstacles to participating in school activities (sports, clubs)
- Increased obstacles to spending face-to-face time with peers
- Trouble returning to regular schooling when that is desired

Children in online school may benefit from a daily schedule that outlines when and how long they will work on each subject. Setting target dates for work completion can also help children in online school keep up a good pace. Some children benefit from a combination of online and in-person classes. Tutoring to help with catching up on content missed from formal instruction may also be helpful. It is important to set realistic goals for your child so that he or she can experience success.

Picking Strategies to Support Your Child's School Goal

Once your child sets a school goal, the next step is to support him or her in reaching this goal. Here we review four strategies that can help: (1) relaxation methods, (2) removing attention on pain, (3) activity pacing, and (4) reward systems.

RELAXATION METHODS

"When I have a pain flare in school," says 16-year-old Alex, who has all-over body pain, "I imagine lying in a towel on the warm white sand of Hawaii. My brother is playing and my dad is watching. I see palm trees swaying. I see the sun through the trees. I hear the crashing of the waves. I smell the ocean's salty water, the blooming flowers, and white sand. I feel the warm breeze and the heated towel wrapped around me."

In Chapter 3 you learned how your child can use relaxation methods such as deep breathing, muscle relaxation, and guided imagery. As you know, relaxation methods can reduce tension and pain and decrease stress. Use of relaxation skills can help your child get to school when he or she has pain in the morning and make it easier for your child to stay in school

> "When I get bad pain during school, I just put my head down and breathe deeply and imagine a relaxing spot."
> —Allie, a 12-year-old-girl with abdominal pain

when there is pain during the day. Your child can also use relaxation skills after school to make it easier to complete homework by reducing stress, pain, and tension.

Here are some tips you can share with your child to help him or her use relaxation strategies at school:

1. If you are sitting at a desk or in a chair, keep your legs and arms uncrossed. This helps your blood circulate in a healthy way.
2. Some children write notes to themselves that they can see during the day, such as on their notebooks, or they use reminders on their cell phones. It can simply read, "Remember to relax." This can help your child to use relaxation strategies during the school day.
3. Deep breathing is easy to use when you are sitting in class without other people noticing what you are doing.
4. Children who don't feel comfortable using relaxation skills in the classroom have found other places to go to relax at school. This could be the front office, the nurse's office, the health room, or the library. Leaving class for 10 minutes to use relaxation skills may help your child spend the rest of the day in school comfortably.
5. Relaxation works best with regular practice, including practice at school, where you want to use the strategy.
6. Even just a few minutes of deep breathing, muscle relaxation, or guided imagery can help reduce the amount of tension and pain your child feels during the school day. Remember, mini-relaxation can be done in only 1 minute.

REMOVE ATTENTION TO PAIN

"Sometimes when I am in pain at school I concentrate really hard on what we are learning and answer a lot of questions. This helps me stay engaged in school and having fun learning. This way I'm not concentrating on the pain."

—Anna, 16-year-old with back pain

Many children and teens find that it is easier to spend time in school when they are doing something that engages their attention so they don't focus on their pain. As Joseph, a 14-year-old with chronic daily headache, told us, "I spend many lunches playing sports or working out to get my mind off of pain that I may have that day." This approach can also give your child something to look forward to during the school day. It turns out that it is much easier to avoid focusing on pain in a busy place like school, where there are many distractions from people and activities.

Scientific studies suggest that altering attention away from pain can reduce it by limiting the number of pain signals processed in the brain. Here are some examples of activities your child or teen might be able to do during scheduled breaks at school (e.g., recess, lunch) to help reduce their focus on pain:

- Talk with a friend
- Read a book or magazine
- Draw
- Play a sports game
- Listen to music (if allowed)
- Play a video game (if allowed)

Here are some tips you can share with your child to help him or her not focus on pain at school:

1. Make an effort to try to focus entirely on something other than how your body feels. Your mind can only pay attention to a certain number of things at one time. When you fully immerse yourself in something else, it is harder to focus on pain.
2. Come to school with items you enjoy. For example, if you enjoy drawing, you could bring paper and drawing pencils.
3. Pay attention to friends and teachers. Listening to someone tell a funny story or concentrating fully on understanding what your teacher is saying can completely engage your attention.
4. Use breaks during the day to do something you enjoy. Spend lunch, recess, or free periods doing those activities that are enjoyable to you.

ACTIVITY PACING

Many teens with chronic pain aren't able to be in school or work on schoolwork as much as they want to. Setting a time limit on activities and taking breaks can help your child spend more time at school. This is called activity pacing. You learned about activity pacing in Chapter 5.

Here are some examples of using activity pacing as part of a school plan:

Melanie knows that she can sit in class for 30 minutes before her pain gets worse. She can set the activity of sitting in class for 30 minutes at a time: Attend class for 30 minutes, rest for 10 minutes (go to the library), attend class for another 30 minutes. Melanie will stop and rest after 30 minutes even if she is in the middle of class. Over time, she will get used to sitting in class and be able to schedule longer periods of time before she needs to rest. Note: Melanie needed to work with her teachers to get permission for this school plan.

Luca knows he can work on homework for 20 minutes before he starts to feel tired and his pain gets worse. He can set the activity of doing homework for 20 minutes at a time: Do homework for 20 minutes, rest for 5 minutes, do homework for another 20 minutes. Luca stops and rests every 20 minutes.

If your child is using activity pacing at school, talk with school staff about whether he or she can go to the nurse's office or library during the rest period and about asking permission to leave class. Eventually, your child may be able to schedule the rest period during a snack or lunch break instead of during class time.

REWARD SYSTEMS

We discussed reward systems in Chapter 4. You can use a reward system to link your child's school goals with rewards. This can help motivate your child to reach school goals.

As you learned from Chapter 4, the key to a successful reward system is to choose realistic goals and to follow through on consequences when the goals are and are not reached. It is important to talk to your child about goals that would be realistic for him or her. It is also important to allow your child to help make the reward system. For example, if the goal is 1 hour of school attendance per day, you can let your child choose what class he or she would like to attend. Of course, you don't want your child going to school for 1 hour a day for the whole year; this is just a starting point. The idea is to help your child have some success at first. Then you can gradually increase your expectations. This will help your child stay motivated

"When my son gets to school on time each day, he can earn 1 hour of computer time at home. If he does not get to school on time, then he does not get access to the computer at home that day."

—Simone, mother of a 16-year-old boy with headaches

to follow the plan. Revisit Chapter 4 for more information on how to make a reward system.

Making a School Plan: Working with School Staff

It is important to communicate with teachers and other school staff about your child's pain problem. Some families want to only share the basics, such as the fact that the child has pain and may miss school. Other families need to share more information because their child needs some extra help to make school more comfortable. It can be useful to ask your child's doctor to provide you with a letter that describes your child's pain condition. You can share this letter with your child's teacher and other school staff.

Here are some accommodations that parents must sometimes request in order to make school easier for children with chronic pain:

- Extra set of textbooks at home
- Reduced class time
- Reduced homework
- Alternatives to physical education class
- In-home tutoring
- Online courses
- Taking the elevator instead of the stairs
- Extra time to complete assignments
- Use of a health room or other quiet space for rest while at school
- Regular check-in meetings with the school counselor

Encourage your child to talk directly to his or her teachers about the pain problem and school plan. This is important, because you will not be with your child during the school day to help carry out the plan. Many teachers like to hear directly from students about problems they are having because it helps them understand what the child is going through from his or her own perspective. Then, it is easier for teachers to help your child succeed in class. Encouraging your child to talk to his or her teachers about the pain problem will also empower your child to learn to manage the pain independently.

Taking Charge at School

"I had perfect attendance. I would get up and go to school. But I wouldn't be able to concentrate very well. By the end of the day, I would have a migraine. I couldn't do my homework. But since I had been in school, my homework would be due the next day. My teachers wouldn't excuse it because I wouldn't tell them I had a migraine. Once I told my teachers what was going on, they were actually very supportive and encouraging. They understood it was better for me to go to school than stay home, even if I felt bad at the end of the day."

—*Jordan, 16-year-old with migraine headaches*

You can also request an in-person meeting with your child's teacher(s) and other school staff (e.g., administrator, school counselor). It is often best if both you and your child attend this meeting. Your child is the only person who knows what types of things would be helpful at school, so by attending the meeting your child can communicate exactly what he or she thinks would make school easier.

A meeting with school staff may also be helpful if you want to ask for special accommodations, such as changing your child's school schedule or getting a second set of textbooks. You can also consider requesting a meeting with school staff if your child is having problems with a certain teacher. For example, one teen with migraines with whom we worked repeatedly asked to be seated away from loud students in the class. He talked to the teacher about his migraines, explaining that he needed less noise. The teacher refused his request to move seats and accused him of faking his pain. The teen's parents met with the teacher and the school counselor, and the decision was made to move the teen to another classroom with a different teacher.

In some countries there are laws about accommodations for students with disabilities, including medical conditions like chronic pain. In the United States, these laws mandate that public schools provide a free and appropriate education to children with disabilities. These laws also mandate that public schools make a plan for how educational goals for children with disabilities will be attained. In the United States, these include Individualized Education Plans (I.E.P.) and Section 504 Plans (504). Children with chronic pain may qualify for one of these plans under the "Other Health Impairments" category. Your child may already have an I.E.P. or 504 Plan for other special needs, such as autism spectrum disorder, learning disability, or emotional or behavioral difficulties. In that case, talk to your child's school counselor about adding accommodations for your child's pain problem to the existing I.E.P. or 504 Plan.

If your child does not have an I.E.P. or 504 Plan, talk to your child's school counselor to find out the steps you need to take to request one. For our patients in U.S. public schools, we always encourage parents to submit this request in writing. The school will then conduct an evaluation to determine whether the child qualifies and, if so, identify accommodations that will benefit the child. Typically, school staff will hold an in-person meeting with parents and the child as part of the evaluation process. It can be very helpful to include in the evaluation a letter from your child's medical provider describing the pain problem and how it impacts the child's academic performance. If your child is working with a psychologist or mental health counselor, that person can also recommend accommodations that may benefit your child. Ask your child's mental health counselor for a letter outlining these recommendations, which you can share with school staff. In certain circumstances, your child's mental health counselor may want to speak with school staff by phone or in person.

> It can be very helpful to have a letter from your child's medical provider describing the pain problem and how it impacts the child's academic performance.

Many of the families we have worked with describe the staff at their school as helpful and eager to support their child in reaching their school goals. For other families we have worked with, building a positive relationship with school staff has been more challenging. In these cases, we have found that it can be helpful to identify one person at the school with whom your child has a positive relationship and involve that person in making your child's school plan. You may also need to compromise on some aspects of the school plan. For example, one family we worked with wanted permission for their 12-year-old to walk on the track at school when he had pain during the school day. The school staff could not allow this because the child would be unsupervised. A compromise was reached where the child was allowed to leave class and walk up and down the hallway for a few minutes. The child found that these walking breaks helped him in working toward his goal of staying in school when he had pain.

Here are some tips for getting support from school staff:

1. Explain that your child might be absent sometimes because of pain.
2. Have a doctor write a note to help explain your child's pain problem.
3. Ask if there is a quiet place your child can go when he or she has pain, like the nurse's office or library.
4. Ask what your child can do to make up work if he or she misses school.
5. If your child has medicine, find out how he or she can bring it to school and where to keep it.

Putting It All Together in a School Plan

Discuss with your child his or her school goals and whether a school plan would be helpful. Talk to your child about how pain interferes with school, and how he or she can work on these things as school goals. Once your child has identified a school goal of his or her own, discuss and identify strategies that your child thinks might help him or her to meet that goal. Talk with your child about whether he or she would want to use relaxation skills, removing focus on pain, activity pacing, reward systems, and/or talking to school staff as part of the school plan. Talk to your child about each strategy, and then you can decide together which of these strategies to include in your child's school plan.

As mentioned, it is important to allow your child to make his or her own school plan. This will make it more likely that your child will follow the plan. After trying out the plan for a week or two, you can then talk to your child about how the plan worked and whether anything should be changed.

Vivienne's School Plan

Vivienne is a 16-year-old girl with abdominal pain. Her abdominal pain typically started during the school day, and most days she would leave school early because of pain. Vivienne's parents were having trouble at work because they often had to leave early to pick Vivienne up from school. Her parents decided to talk to her about her school goals and what they could do to help her be more comfortable in school. As they talked, Vivienne shared that she was tired of missing school and that she also missed her friends. She wanted to make a goal of staying in school for as many hours as she could over the next month. Together, Vivienne and her parents came up with several steps to help her reach this goal:

1. They made a school plan for increasing time at school. Vivienne had learned deep breathing from her mother and was open to trying it at school. She also wanted a second set of textbooks so she didn't have to carry books with her at school. Her parents offered to give her rewards for staying in school, and Vivienne was excited about this.
2. Vivienne and her parents met with her teachers to talk about some changes that would make staying in school easier. She got permission to have a second set of textbooks. She also was able to rest in the library at any time to use her deep-breathing skills.
3. Vivienne and her parents worked together to make a reward system that rewarded her for staying in school. Her parents talked to her about things she wanted to earn, and they set realistic goals.
4. Vivienne followed through on her plan. She pushed herself to stay in school even when she had pain.

When Vivienne first started working on her goal to spend more time in school it was not easy. She kept having pain at school, and her family wasn't sure what to do. Once she and her parents started to follow her school plan, staying in school got easier. Over time, many positive things started happening at school. Vivienne was invited to go more places with her friends, and her grades improved. These positive outcomes helped Vivienne stay motivated to stick with her plan, so her school attendance improved.

School Refusal and School Re-entry

Some children with chronic pain may refuse to go to school because they do not feel well. They may refuse to go to school as soon as they wake up, or they may go to school at the beginning of the day but ask to come home early. Extreme and emotional behaviors may make it hard to manage children's school refusal. For example, a child may scream and cry in the morning, begging to stay home from school.

Some children with chronic pain may be out of school for a long time before a doctor (usually a pain specialist) tells them it is okay to go back. Getting a child to go back to school after a long absence can be hard. Children who have been out of school for a long time may feel overwhelmed by the amount of catch-up work that is due, or they may worry about what their friends or teachers think about their absence, feeling isolated from their classmates.

When children or teens have missed 2 or more months of school in a given school year, they may have difficulty succeeding academically when they return because of gaps in instruction. In particular, children who miss a lot of school may have trouble excelling in subjects like math and science, for which skills build on one another over time. It is important to talk to your child's school counselor about how to make up missed work and to determine whether he or she is on track to move on to the next grade. This is especially important for high school

> Children who have been out of school for a long time may feel overwhelmed by catch-up work, or they may worry about what their friends or teachers think about their absence.

students who have course credit requirements in order to graduate. The school counselor may recommend making up missed credits during summer school, or repeating classes during the next school year. Your family may also want to consider hiring a tutor to help your child catch up on missed work.

For children who have been out of school for a long time, it may be helpful to begin to work on school re-entry by setting up a practice school day in your home. This would require your child to complete schoolwork at a desk or table at home. At first, you may need to start with very short periods of time spent on schoolwork, such as 5 or 10 minutes—whatever your child feels like he or she could do to start out. The key is to pick a realistic goal to start with and then gradually work to increase the time your child spends on schoolwork. Once your child is able to spend a few hours sitting in a chair comfortably to do schoolwork at home, you can consider your home practice complete. Then it is time to try spending time at school.

Here are some tips for school re-entry:

1. Set reasonable goals. If your child has been out of school for a long time, it may make the most sense to start with a part-time schedule. Depending on what your child can tolerate, you may want to start with as little as 1 hour a day. It is important to start out with a goal that your child will be able to reach.

2. Gradually increase your expectation for school attendance. Again, you want to set goals that your child will be able to reach. At the same time, you don't want your child to be in school for only 1 hour a day for the entire year. The best way to increase your child's time in school is to do it gradually. For example, say you start out with a goal of 1 hour per day. Once your child does this for 5 days in a row, you can increase the goal to 2 hours per day. You can increase by an hour per day each week until your child is back in school full time. You can evaluate this plan every week with your child to see how it is working and if you need to make any changes.

3. Involve your child in making a plan to go back to school. This will make it more likely that your child will follow the plan.

4. If your child has been out of school for a long time, talk with your child about what he or she will say to teachers and other kids about where he or she has been. You can practice this with

your child. Having a plan for what to say can help your child feel less worried about returning to school.

5. Communicate with school staff. Earlier in this chapter you learned about specific strategies for how to get support from school staff.

Casey, a 14-Year-Old Girl with Abdominal Pain Who Refused to Go to School

At first, Casey's mother allowed her to stay home from school so that she could rest, but Casey's abdominal pain continued and worsened. After a few months, Casey saw a gastroenterologist and was diagnosed with functional abdominal pain. Her doctors advised that she return to school even if she still had pain. This was hard for Casey and her mother to understand at first. However, Casey's mother recognized that missing school was not helping Casey's pain.

Casey and her mother talked to her school counselor about her options. The school counselor agreed to put a Section 504 plan in place to help Casey get back into school. Casey decided she would start out by attending school for 1 hour per day at lunchtime. Casey attended the lunch period for an entire week and it was a big success. Casey then agreed to try attending school for half-days. Her mother also made a reward system in which Casey would earn the privilege of using her cell phone only on days that she went to school. She could also earn fingernail polish for going to school every day for a week.

On the first day of this new plan, Casey was excited and went to school without difficulty. The second day was more challenging. She woke up complaining of abdominal pain and nausea. She refused to get out of bed, then cried and begged her mother to allow her to stay home. Her mother found it very difficult to see Casey so upset, but Casey did not have a fever, so her mother stayed firm in her expectation that Casey get up and go to school. That day, Casey made it to school 1 hour late.

Things continued this way for a while. Over time, Casey began to experience success at school. Her grades started to improve, she reconnected with her friends, and she became involved in the school play. She still had abdominal pain but had an easier time going to school and staying in school when she had pain. By the end of the year, she was attending school full-time.

Friendships: Strategies to Support Your Child's Social Relationships

When children miss school and other activities, they can start to be left out of plans by friends. Friends may stop asking your child to do things because they are used to hearing that he or she is sick or can't participate in the activity. It can be important for your child to talk to friends about the pain problem. You can help your child figure out what to say so that his or her friends will understand, and then practice this conversation with your child. You can also ask a doctor for guidance on what to say. Communicating directly about the problem will help your child's friends understand why your child sometimes misses school or other activities. Friends are more likely to be supportive and understanding if they know about the pain problem and how it impacts your child's life. Your child can also share with his or her friends the strategies that help with managing the pain so that they can help your child use these strategies at school. For example, your child could ask friends to help keep him or her distracted during lunch, by telling funny stories or playing a game. If your child wants to spend more time in school, he or she can share this goal with friends and they can then encourage your child to stay in school when he or she has pain.

Sometimes friendships need to change because of the pain problem. Children may not have opportunities to be around the same peers if they are no longer involved with sports and other extracurricular activities. They may simply not have anything in common any longer. For example, if your child used to play basketball and hang out with friends who also played basketball, then this peer group may not be the right fit any more. Children may need to develop new friendships, and this can be a challenge.

You can include your child's friendship goals in his or her school plan. For example, you could have a school plan that targets attending school 3 days a week and playing soccer 3 days a week. Your school plan could also focus on participating in new after-school clubs or activities in order to make new friends.

Here are some tips for supporting your child's friendships:

1. Encourage your child to give friends information about the pain problem. Talk to your child about how to explain the pain problem in a way his or her friends will understand. Some children find it helpful to start by sharing with their closest friend(s) first.
2. Encourage your child to keep in touch with friends when he or she is absent. It is important to talk to at least one friend every day by phone, text message, e-mail, or social networking. Talking to friends every day will make it easier for your child to return to school.
3. If your child has to cancel an activity with friends, encourage him or her to let them know as soon as possible. Friends will be more understanding if they know what he or she is going through. They will be less understanding if your child simply doesn't show up without an explanation.
4. Encourage your child to develop new friendships. If your child's interests and activities have changed, he or she may find that old friendships are more difficult to maintain. And, new friends with whom your child can socially connect will always be a welcome addition even if he or she rekindles old friendships later on.

Bullying

Thinking back, most adults can remember negative interactions with peers growing up. In fact, it is typical for children to experience isolated acts of peer aggression (rumor spreading, exclusion, threats, physical or verbal attacks) at some point in childhood. Nevertheless, all complaints about bullying should be taken seriously by parents. Peer aggression is especially concerning when the acts are meant to be hurtful, if the child is a frequent target, or both.

It can be helpful to talk to children about how they feel about their friendships, starting at a young age, including setting expectations regarding friendships and how to recognize and respond to bullying that occurs both in person and online. You may also model your own positive relationships and create opportunities to spend time with kids who are likely to have positive relationships with your child. Research shows that having one good-quality friendship can protect against the effects of bullying, loneliness, and depression.

> Having one good-quality friendship can protect against the effects of bullying, loneliness, and depression.

It is also important to talk to your child about appropriate use of computer technology and online safety. You can teach your child to tell a trusted adult and gather evidence and document the incidents if he or she or a friend is being bullied online. Depending on your child's age and social relationships, you may need to balance your child's desire for privacy with necessary monitoring and supervision of his or her Internet activities.

If asked directly by a parent about whether they are being bullied, most children will say they are not. Many children will deny that they are being mistreated by other kids because it is embarrassing and they may be afraid of personal consequences for them if they admit to it. To get an accurate assessment of the kinds of peer problems your child might be experiencing, it is better to ask whether specific behaviors or situations have happened to him or her. For example, you can ask about situations such as not being invited to outings or events that your child wanted to go to, or someone making rude or mean comments about your child on social media. Helping your child to problem-solve these situations will increase your child's sense of control and support his or her developing independence. You will learn more about problem-solving skills in Chapter 8.

Developing a relationship with your child's school staff is important if you are concerned that your child is being bullied. Most schools have clearly established procedures for responding to complaints about bullying at school or online. You can talk to your child's school counselor for more information about how the school responds to negative peer interactions and how they can help you and your child handle these situations.

Guilt About Pushing Your Child to Go to School When in Pain

As a parent, pushing your child to go to school when he or she is in severe pain can be emotionally challenging. No parent wants to watch his or her child suffer. Many parents feel guilty about taking their child to school when the child does not feel well. Your child may also say that school makes the pain worse, which can add to the guilt and bad feelings. When facing these emotional challenges, it is important to keep in mind that attending school will help your child in the long term. In our experience, children often start to experience less pain as they are able to spend more time in school. However, it can take several months for this to occur. For some children, their pain may not change, but they will begin to experience success in other ways (e.g., improved grades, friendships, participation in sports and clubs).

As a parent or caregiver, it is important for you to also get support. It may be helpful to talk to your spouse, a close friend, or a family member about your thoughts and feelings about working with your child on school goals. Many parents tell us that they have needed to keep a sense of humor and keep some perspective so that they can better face the challenges of working on school issues.

Summary

From this chapter you learned how pain can interfere with school. You learned several strategies that can help your child reach his or her school goals: relaxation methods, removing attention on pain, activity pacing, and reward systems. You learned how to make a school plan, how to get support from school staff, and how to support your child's social relationships. Implementing a school plan may be hard at first. As your child reaches his or her initial school goals, you can increase the challenge by adding additional goals.

Chapter 7 Practice Assignment

Practice using a school plan to help your child reach his or her school goals. Using the examples in this chapter, talk to your child about his or her school goals and what would help your child to reach those goals. Make the school plan specific. You may need to communicate with school staff so that they are aware of your child's pain problem and the school plan. If you want to make a formal request for accommodations, talk to your child's school counselor about the best way to do this. Once you start the school plan, be sure to give it enough time so that you can assess how it is working. At the end of the first week, decide if the plan is helping your child to reach his or her school goals. Was your child able to reach the goals that he or she set? Was your child able to talk to friends and school staff?

List your child's school goals here:

1. _____

2. _____

3. _____

List the strategies you and your child will use to reach these goals:

1. _____

2. _____

3. _____

4. _____

5. _____

You may decide that the school plan is working well and continue with it as it is. Or, you may decide that you need to make some changes to the school plan. If you change the school plan, you can re-evaluate after another week to see if it is working better. As your child reaches the goals he or she chose, you may think of other school goals you want to encourage your child to work on.

Coping with Pain, Stress, and Other Problems

Liz's daughter Erika has chronic widespread musculoskeletal pain. Liz also has a history of chronic pain; she has struggled with fibromyalgia over the past 12 years. When she notices Erika having painful symptoms, Liz feels that she understands exactly what her daughter is going through. However, she has come to realize that it is very difficult for her to encourage Erika to push through the pain and use coping strategies because of her own experience with chronic pain.

THE GOAL OF THIS CHAPTER IS FOR YOU TO LEARN HOW TO MODEL positive coping strategies for your child. We will review how children learn methods of coping with pain, stress, and other problems by observing adults, and provide suggestions for how to model helpful methods of coping. You will also learn several positive coping skills, including problem-solving skills and strategies to deal with negative thoughts that can reduce your own stress.

Modeling

Your child has learned many things simply from watching you. Humans have an amazing ability to learn just by watching others. Children are particularly good at this because their brains are still developing and they are always actively learning about their environments. By extension, it is normal for children to imitate their parent's behavior. Think of things you have seen your child do that remind you of yourself, such as facial expressions, how your child stands or carries him- or herself, or how your child performs a task. You may recognize some positive mannerisms, such as politeness or social graces. On the other hand, you will probably also recognize some negative mannerisms, such as rude or inappropriate expressions. Many parents recall watching their toddler imitate a foul expression or obscenity that sounds exactly the same as when the parent used the same word. A toddler uses profanity after dropping his or her teddy bear—this is an obvious example of learning (in this case, an obscenity) and how to use it (e.g., in times of anger).

It is essential that parents show their children positive coping behaviors as much as possible.

Though imitation is a normal part of learning for every child, for the child with chronic pain, modeling or learning through observation can be particularly important. Children may observe adults using either helpful or unhelpful methods of coping with pain, stress, and other problems. Since children may imitate the adult behaviors they observe, it is essential that parents show their children positive coping behaviors as much as possible. These are opportunities for children to observe and imitate helpful rather than unhelpful behaviors.

You Are Your Child's Most Powerful Role Model for Coping with Pain and Stress

Parents are particularly powerful role models for children, for several reasons. First, your child sees you nearly every day and spends considerable time around you. This provides many opportunities for observing and imitating behaviors. Second, your child sees you engage in many important daily-life activities. Normal day-to-day life provides many chances to model how to cope, relate with others, and solve problems. Third, your child has spent many years looking to you to know right from wrong. Your child trusts your opinions because you know him or her better than most other people. For these reasons, modeling positive coping and sharing useful problem-solving strategies with your child may lead to your child learning to use these types of helpful strategies by him- or herself.

Here is a list of common situations in which parents have the opportunity to model positive coping strategies. These can become teaching moments in your day-to-day life. Think about the types of behaviors you show when you

- Make mistakes
- Experience stress or worries
- Have to make difficult decisions
- Need to be assertive
- Experience pain
- Have disappointments
- Receive bad news
- Interact with friends

Of course, everyone displays both positive and negative coping strategies in different situations. None of us would want to be evaluated on the basis of each and every situation and the resulting behaviors we show. For example, certain mistakes can be really intolerable and you may demonstrate negative behaviors (e.g., extreme anger, self-criticism). This is a normal part of coping. The important thing is that your child also sees that you can cope using positive strategies in different situations. Even if you recognize that you have demonstrated many negative coping strategies in the past, you still have a great opportunity now to show your child other positive coping strategies.

Some Examples of Modeling

Will (father to 14-year-old Caroline) is worried because he has been waiting to hear the outcome of his mother's surgery. He is nervous that his mother's cancer will not be successfully removed by surgery. Here are some different ways he might model how he handles stress and anticipation. Think about what Will is modeling in each of these examples. What would

Caroline be learning that she should do when she is stressed or anxious?

1. During dinner, Will says, "I am so stressed about everything, I really need a drink."
2. Will begins to yell at the kids to pick up their school bags and papers on the kitchen table. He then apologizes and says, "I'm sorry, I'm just really stressed about Grandma."
3. After dinner, Will leaves the kitchen and says, "I need a few minutes to myself. I'm really nervous about Grandma's surgery and I want to relax a little."
4. When Caroline asks for a ride to her friend's house, Will says, "Why do I always have to drive you everywhere?"

In the third example, Will is teaching his children to use positive coping strategies such as relaxation and asserting needs appropriately when feeling stressed. The other examples are less healthy ways of coping that involve withdrawal from activities, unhelpful strategies such as alcohol, and demonstrating an inability to deal with emotional upset.

What if a Parent or Caregiver Has a Pain Problem Too?

Modeling may also be very specific to how we cope with pain. Many adults have problems with pain. It may be the same type of pain problem that your child has or it may be a different type of pain. Research studies have found that children are more likely to have a problem with pain when one or both caregivers also have a pain problem, so children often learn how to act when in pain from watching how adults act when they are in pain. For example, a parent who has migraine headaches may show a range of coping behaviors for dealing with the headache, such as taking medication, sleeping, or relaxing. The parent may also behave in various ways in response to the headache, such as whether or not to go to work, and whether or not to participate in family activities that day. Children also learn about emotional responses to pain from their parents. When parents become very emotionally distressed by pain, children may learn that they should also be distressed by pain.

Your child will learn the most positive and helpful ways of coping by seeing adults doing the following when they experience pain:

- Show confidence in their ability to cope
- Use positive coping strategies (e.g., relaxation, stretching, positive self-talk)
- Continue to do their usual activities
- Stay calm

TALKING TO YOUR CHILD ABOUT HOW YOU COPE WITH STRESS AND PAIN

As mentioned, the simple act of watching or observing another person is one way to learn. However, one of the best ways to teach something new to a child is to show him or her how to work toward a challenging goal and to talk through your approach. For example, your child may watch you try to open a jar with your hand, and then when it doesn't open easily, see that you use a butter knife to hit the lid of the jar. A verbal explanation (you talking through the approach) can help your child understand how you approached the problem. This can look like a running commentary or a simple statement of the methods you are using. Your child will learn to try different or multiple methods in order to cope successfully with a situation. Speaking your thoughts aloud will show your child how to think through a particular problem or situation.

> Speaking your thoughts aloud will show your child how to think through a particular problem or situation.

Most parents don't share all of their thoughts with their teens, which is appropriate the vast majority of the time. Sharing too much can be detrimental when it puts you on the same level as your child and undermines your authority as a parent. However, it is a special circumstance when you are teaching your child coping skills. What you show your child can help him or her cope with pain. Of course, you don't want to share all of your problems with your child. At the same time, it can be helpful to talk to your child about how you cope with stress and pain.

"In times of stress, I try to model slowing down and doing something quietly that makes me feel calm, like listening to music, having a cup of tea, or gardening. I encouraged her to find what brings her serenity and peace."
—*Linda, mother of a 15-year-old girl with abdominal pain*

It is also important to monitor how much distress you demonstrate to your child. Some parents may find themselves in tears when they accompany their child to doctors' appointments. Other parents may act like everything is fine and refuse to talk about their feelings, even though they feel that everything is wrong. These are common reactions for parents who care for a child with medical problems. However, they are not helpful models for teaching your child to tolerate stress. Think about how you would like your child to see you coping with stress and worries. One of the assignments in this chapter will be to monitor (track) your behavior to see if there are more positive coping strategies you can share with your child.

For example, Jonah's father Tom has back pain that can be very severe at times. One morning, Tom woke up with a lot of back pain. He modeled coping by simply talking about his thoughts. He said to Jonah, "My back is killing me this morning. I thought about calling in sick, but I don't want to miss work. I'll try my back stretches and see if I can feel better by the time I need to leave." Normally, Tom would cope with his back pain without describing this process aloud to Jonah. Talking to Jonah about the strategies he will use to get to work despite his pain is a great opportunity to model positive coping. Just talking with your child about the different options available for solving problems or for coping with pain can be helpful. This teaches your child that pain doesn't have to stop everything. Your child also learns that it is normal to try multiple solutions to reach a goal.

Problem-Solving Skills

Research shows that effective problem-solving can reduce stress among parents of children with chronic medical conditions. As discussed in Chapter 1, children and teens with chronic pain whose parents are more stressed tend to have more pain and worse functioning. Reducing your stress can help you feel more in control of your life, and may also help your child cope better with pain. You can also model these skills for your child or teen so that he or she can learn an effective way for solving problems in his or her own life.

A lot of research has gone into determining the best ways to teach people to solve problems; in fact, this has been studied for decades. We are going to teach you the method of solving problems that has been shown to be most effective. You can learn more about this approach from the book *Solving Life's Problems: A 5-Step Guide to Enhanced Well-Being*, by Arthur Nezu, Christine Nezu, and Thomas D'Zurilla (see the Resources and Bibliography section of this book).

There are six steps to solving problems:

1. Have an optimistic attitude
2. State the problem
3. Brainstorm solutions
4. Evaluate your options
5. Try out your solution
6. Decide how it worked

The idea behind learning this approach to solving problems is to help you manage the stress that goes along with the demands of caring for a child with chronic pain. You will be better able to handle conflicts; make more informed decisions; effectively manage your time; and solve family, school-related, and other problems using these techniques. Consequently, you will become less stressed, more relaxed, and calm and feel more in control. You will be able to spend more time and energy in ways that more effectively support your child with his or her pain management needs.

Step 1: Have an Optimistic Attitude

Optimism is key to solving problems effectively. It means acknowledging the impact that pain has on your family and recognizing that things can and will get better. It means believing that you *can* solve problems and overcome challenges. Optimism also involves understanding that the problems you are facing with your child's chronic pain are normal and expected. Conflicts, problems, and decisions are a daily part of your child's and family's life; they are common to

How a person thinks about problems can greatly influence the way he or she actually copes with difficulties.

all families going through this experience. How a person thinks about problems can greatly influence the way he or she actually copes with difficulties. This also affects the amount of stress experienced in the process. Later in this chapter you will learn a few strategies that will help you to be more optimistic. These include positive coping statements, thought stopping, and thought restructuring.

Step 2: State the Problem

Problems may not always be easy to recognize. Sometimes it is easy to recognize the negative consequences of a problem, but we aren't clear on what the actual problem is. There are several aids for increasing your ability to recognize problems:

1. Use your **feelings** as a clue that a problem exists. The negative feelings (e.g., sadness, frustration, anger) aren't the problem; they are a *signal* that a real problem is causing these negative feelings.
2. Use your **behavior** as a signal that a problem exists. If you are making mistakes over and over or your responses just aren't effective, then this is another clue that a problem exists.
3. Use **certain types of thoughts** as clues that problems exist. Strong thoughts that include the words *never, always, should,* or *must* are often indicators that a problem exists and that it is time to take a step back and consider what your alternatives may be.
4. Use a **problem checklist**. This can be a way to pinpoint specific problems. Review the checklist of common problems for parents of children with chronic pain, found in Chapter 1.

Step 3: Brainstorm Solutions

The next step is to define your options by brainstorming potential solutions to the problem. Many people stop themselves from solving problems by saying they have no alternatives, that the problem can't be solved because there are no good solutions, or that they have already tried everything. You may have problems on your list that you have tried to solve before without success. You may feel like you have already tried everything. If you notice that you are feeling this way, we want you to *be creative*. Brainstorming solutions involves stretching yourself. Remember, new ways of solving old problems are always worth trying out.

A key step in brainstorming is to avoid judging yourself or the solutions you are coming up with. If you find that you can't think of any solutions, try writing down things that seem really out of the box. These can be things you would never actually try in real life. The important thing is to write down everything that comes to your mind without judging whether it will work or not. This will help you come up with a good variety of solutions to consider in the next step.

Use Appendix G to develop a list of potential solutions to the problem you have identified. Think up as many alternative solutions as you can and write them down. We want you to think of at least 10 possible solutions. Remember, be creative!

One of the greatest barriers to developing new and effective solutions is habit. Your child has had pain for a long time and it is likely that you and your family have developed habits for dealing with it. It is easy to get stuck in the same old rut of trying to solve a problem in the same old way. Doing what you've always done is familiar and easy to do, but it can often be ineffective. Remember: There are alternative solutions to even the most difficult problems.

Once you have made your list of possible solutions, rate each one. Ask yourself the following questions:

- Will this solution solve the problem?
- Can I really carry it out?
- What are the overall effects on **me** (short and long term)?
- What are the overall effects on **others** (short and long term)?

You should think about whether your answer is generally positive (by putting a + sign for the item), generally negative (by putting a − [minus] sign for the item), or neutral (by putting a 0 for the item). For example, some solutions may have really negative consequences for you, and you would indicate this on the worksheet by putting a − sign in the column "overall effects on me." The worksheet in Appendix G provides a way to help define the solutions in a way that will make it easier to choose the one you think will work best.

Step 4: Evaluate Your Options

Once you have completed the brainstorming step, you can evaluate your options and choose your best solution. Look at each choice on your list on Worksheet 1. Screen each one based on the following:

- **Eliminate** right away any solutions that have too many risks or negative consequences. These are the solutions with lots of −'s (minus signs). Cross these solutions off the list.
- **Select** two or three good possible solutions and circle them. Think about any possible barriers to these solutions. Rank your solutions from best to worst.

Step 5: Try Out Your Solution

After you have ranked your solutions, choose a solution to try. Make a detailed action plan to outline exactly how you are going to carry out the chosen solution. Real-life problems are complex. It is likely that multiple things are making the situation a problem. Part of the task with large problems is breaking them down into smaller ones. It can be important to list the small steps you will need to take in order to reach the larger goal of solving the problem. Your action plan may need to combine multiple solutions (that is, several different smaller steps with different solutions). Once you have made your action plan, it is time to carry it out.

Step 6: Decide if It Worked

After you carry out the action plan, decide if your plan gives you a result you are satisfied with. If you are not completely satisfied with the result, then troubleshoot the reasons why. This step tells you where you have gone right or wrong. It is important to know that factors other than what you are doing may impact the results of your action plan (like how other people respond to the plan, for example). You may have to modify your action plan or even try out your next choice. If solution #2 is not satisfactory either, try solution #3 or go back to earlier problem-solving steps and make certain that you defined the problem correctly.

An Example of Problem Solving: Katherine's Story

My name is Katherine and my daughter, Melissa, is 16 years old. She has very bad headaches that happen almost every single day. Sometimes it feels like her headaches affect everyone in the family and everything we do as a family. It's really frustrating.

STEP 1: HAVE AN OPTIMISTIC ATTITUDE

The first step is for Katherine to have optimism—specifically, seeing problems as normal, ordinary, inevitable parts of life. Katherine will try to perceive the problem as a challenge or opportunity and know that while it might take time and effort, she believes there is a solution to the problem she is trying to solve.

Katherine creates a few positive self-statements to help achieve and keep a positive orientation:

> *Sometimes it seems like our situation with Melissa's headaches is never going to change. I am, however, hopeful that things might get better for us as a family and there will be an end to this difficulty.*

STEP 2: STATE THE PROBLEM

The second step is for Katherine to clearly identify the problem she wants to address. Katherine thinks about the issues going on in her life as she works through the list of common problems in families coping with chronic pain, presented in Table 1.1 in Chapter 1. She checks off some problems that other parents who have children with chronic pain experience, as well as noting some of her own.

Here is Katherine's list of problems:

- I can't get my child to go to school or to other activities.
- I'm worried my child won't graduate.
- I can't get my child to do chores.
- I worry more than ever now.
- I worry about how much to push my child.
- I'm worried that my child will never get better.
- My life feels like it is falling apart.

- I have trouble sleeping.
- Our family doesn't get along well any more.
- We aren't talking a lot lately.
- This situation is putting strain on my marriage.
- I get very angry waiting for so long to talk to the doctor for just a few minutes.

Katherine writes down the problems she would like to work on solving.

> Problem #1: *I argue too often with my husband about how to deal with Melissa's pain.*
> Problem #2: *I'm concerned Melissa won't get into any good colleges.*
> Problem #3: *I have a hard time falling asleep and never feel rested.*

Katherine picks a problem she wants to work on and is very specific about what the problem is. The first problem to be solved is this one:

> *Melissa's headaches have made it really hard for her to go to school regularly and to keep up on her schoolwork. Because she is in high school we are worried about what effect this is going to have on her chances of getting into good colleges. My husband and I have been struggling a lot with this. Every morning my husband and I fight about whether to make Melissa go to school and which one of us will have to wake her up.*

STEP 3: BRAINSTORM SOLUTIONS

The third step is for Katherine to figure out what to do to make changes happen. That is, she needs to brainstorm all of the possible solutions. By coming up with many different solutions, Katherine increases the chances of finding the best one.

Katherine brainstorms as many possible solutions to this problem as she can. See Table 8.1 for her list. She comes up with some solutions she has already tried for the problem and generates as many new ideas as she can think of. Katherine tries not to limit herself, so she writes down all possible solutions—even those that she knows seem ridiculous.

STEP 4: EVALUATE YOUR OPTIONS

In Step 4, Katherine will evaluate the options she came up with and decide which is best for her. Most importantly, she has to decide what the barriers are. Are there things on her list that she is not willing to do? Are there things that she thinks probably won't work? Are there things that are more trouble than it's worth to try to change? This is a *cost–benefit analysis*. Is the cost (what one has to change) worth the benefit (the problem getting better or becoming less of an issue)?

Katherine evaluates the list she came up with. She crosses off some options right away because she knows they are things she is not willing to do, such as:

- Sleep in a different room than my husband so that I don't have to talk about this with him every morning
- Throw cold water on Melissa to wake her up
- Make Jacob, our youngest child, be in charge of waking up Melissa
- Homeschool her, or have her do an online school
- Tell Melissa not to go to sleep so she doesn't have to wake up
- Get a divorce so my husband and I don't argue any more
- Make lots of noise in the morning (bang pots and pans) to wake Melissa

Based on the costs and benefits, Katherine evaluates the remaining options and ranks them. Katherine has evaluated the pros, cons, and barriers of all of the options. She decides to try taking away Melissa's cell phone if she doesn't go to school. She knows that Melissa loves having a cell phone and would be upset if she couldn't use it. Katherine thinks Melissa would be motivated to get up and go to school if she implements this plan.

STEP 5: TRY OUT YOUR SOLUTION

Step 5 is to try out your solution. After you've chosen the solution you're going to try, create a *detailed action plan* showing specifically how you are going to implement your choice. Write down your action plan and try it out!

TABLE 8.1 Example: Katherine's Brainstorming Worksheet

List possible solutions (Be creative!)	Will this solution solve the problem?	Can I really carry it out?	What are the overall effects on **me** (short and long term)?	What are the overall effects on **others** (short and long term)?
1. My husband takes full responsibility for dealing with Melissa every morning.	0	0	+/0	–
2. Ignore the problem and don't try to make her go to school.	–	–	–	0
3. Talk to the school about letting Melissa start at a later time so she can sleep in.	0	0	0	0
4. Let Melissa decide on her own whether to go to school.	–	+	–	–
5. Take turns with my husband—alternate days we are responsible for getting her to get up and go to school.	0	+	0/+	0/+
6. Sleep in a different room than my husband so that I don't have to talk or argue about it with him.	–	–	–	–
7. Throw cold water on Melissa to wake her up.	–	+	–	–

8. Have Melissa set an alarm clock to wake herself each morning for school.	0	+	+	+
9. Make Jacob, our youngest child, be in charge of waking up Melissa.	0	0	0	–
10. Give Melissa rewards (e.g., iTunes gift-card) for waking up to go to school	0	+	+/–	0
11. Take away Melissa's cell phone if she doesn't go to school.	+	+	0	0
12. Give Melissa one chance a week to stay home from school—she can pick the day.	0	0	0	–
13. Quit my job and homeschool her.	–	–	–	–
14. Tell Melissa not to go to sleep so she doesn't have to wake up.	–	–	–	–
15. Get a divorce from my husband so we don't argue any more.	–	–	–	–
16. Make lots of noise in the morning (bang pots and pans) to wake Melissa.	–	+	0/–	0/–

Rate (+ = generally positive, – = generally negative, 0 = neutral)

Katherine has decided to try taking away Melissa's cell phone if she doesn't get up in the morning and go to school. She creates a detailed plan for how she will act out each step:

Action plan: I will try this plan for 1 week of school. Each night after dinner I will remind Melissa that if she doesn't get up and go to school in the morning I will take her cell phone for the day. If she doesn't get up the next morning and go to school I will immediately take her phone and keep it in my desk until the next morning.

Katherine put her plan into action. Here's what happened:

Action tried: On Sunday I told Melissa that if she didn't get up the next morning and go to school I would take her cell phone for the day. She wasn't happy and slammed her bedroom door. Monday morning Melissa didn't get up for school. My husband and I argued about who would go into her room, wake her up, and take her cell phone. I had to go in and wake her up and take her cell phone. Melissa cried and yelled at me but did go to school on the bus. She was still angry at me when she got home from school. Tuesday morning Melissa got up, but said she had a really bad headache—an 8 or 9 pain level. My husband and I argued about whether she had to go to school. Melissa didn't go to school and we didn't take her cell phone. Wednesday morning I woke up late, and my husband had to wake Melissa up, but he didn't take her phone away. We argued about taking the phone away—I was so tired, I gave in and let Melissa keep it. I didn't even bring it up on Thursday or Friday.

STEP 6: DECIDE IF IT WORKED

Step 6 helps you see whether the plan is working well or if you need to make some changes. Decide if your plan gives you a solution you are satisfied with. If you are not completely satisfied with the result, then troubleshoot the reasons why. You may have to modify your plan or even try out another solution.

After putting her plan in action, Katherine looks back on the week to see how well it worked.

Results—see if it worked: On Monday my plan kind of worked because Melissa went to school, but my husband and I still wound up arguing. On Tuesday she didn't go to school, but she still kept her cell phone and my husband and I argued about it. On Wednesday my plan definitely didn't work.

Katherine is not satisfied with how things went. The problem she wanted to address was: "My husband and I fight every morning about whether to make Melissa go to school." After trying to take Melissa's phone away, she found that she and her husband were arguing just as much as before and that it wasn't effective for getting Melissa to school.

Katherine thinks more about how the week went and decides that taking Melissa's phone away is not worth trying again. Instead, she looks back at her list of possible solutions and adds a couple of new possibilities. *She recognizes that the problem has multiple parts and may need more than one solution.* Katherine decides that she will try having Melissa set an alarm. She will also try rewarding her for going to school. And, she will try deep breathing to help reduce her high emotions in the situation. This time she will try implementing these three solutions together.

Katherine considers a specific action plan. She starts with planning a detailed conversation with her husband about how they will work on this plan *together.* Katherine decides that she will share her solution list with her husband and talk about how she came up with the new plan. On Saturday, Katherine will go to the store with Melissa to buy an alarm clock for Melissa's room. They will also buy an iTunes gift card that Melissa can earn at the end of the week if she gets up for school and goes at least four days of the week. On Sunday she will help Melissa set an alarm for 6:30 A.M., which gives Melissa enough time to shower and get ready for school with a little extra time to spare. Each school night she and her husband will remind Melissa to set her alarm.

On Saturday Katherine starts acting out her plan by first having the conversation with her husband. Katherine also committed to practicing deep breathing for a few minutes each day so that she can use this strategy to reduce her high negative emotions.

Katherine looks back on how the second week went. Monday she and her husband heard Melissa's alarm go off three times, but Melissa got out of bed before Katherine or her husband went to wake her. Tuesday morning Melissa's alarm didn't go off because Melissa forgot to set it. Katherine and her husband argued about who had to wake her up. Katherine used deep breathing to help herself to not get as upset. On Tuesday night, Katherine was sure to remind Melissa to set her alarm. On Wednesday morning Melissa got up after the alarm went off the second time. Thursday and Friday morning Melissa was very grumpy when her alarm went off, but got up before Katherine or her husband went into her room. Melissa earned the iTunes gift card on Friday afternoon and seemed pleased with it.

Katherine believes this week went much better. Even though she and her husband still argued, it was much less than before. And, importantly, Melissa got to school four days out of the week by waking by herself. Katherine noticed that she felt more like a team with her husband. They observed together that reminding Melissa to set her alarm helped and that Melissa was happy with earning a reward. They decided to keep this plan in place for the next few weeks.

Dealing with Negative Thoughts

This next section focuses on negative thoughts and several strategies that can be used to help reduce negative thoughts. We present this section because having negative thoughts often increases stress, and these skills can help you to reduce your own stress.

We all have negative thoughts at times. We may worry about what a person thinks of something we said or did; we may worry about the outcome of an event; or we may not be able to get a negative interaction or conversation out of our thoughts. All of these negative thoughts can lead to negative feelings, including stress, depressed mood, and tension, which can make pain worse. We know that stress experienced by parents is important to address because it can lead to depression and anxiety. Also, daily hassles and stress often get in the way of effective behavior change. By using positive coping strategies that reduce negative thoughts, you might experience a reduction in stress, and reducing your own stress may help your child to cope better.

> Negative thoughts can lead to negative feelings, including stress, depressed mood, and tension, which can make pain worse.

A special type of negative thought that can get in the way and lead to negative feelings is known as *catastrophizing*. This is the type of thought that makes us worry that an extremely bad thing will happen, often due to a smaller thing that has already happened. We have all survived thoughts of catastrophe and we know that not all worrisome events come true. This is an important principle that underlies the use of these coping strategies. Thoughts are just thoughts. They don't make something happen, and they may or may not come true. Three strategies to deal with negative thoughts are described in this section: 1) replacing negative thoughts, 2) positive self-statements, and 3) thought STOPping.

Replacing Negative Thoughts

One strategy for reducing negative thoughts is to replace them with more reasonable or positive thoughts. For example, a parent may think, "My teen's pain will never go away." One way to recognize that this is a negative thought is the extremeness of it (use of the word "never") and to consider the feelings that go along with that. For this parent, the thought brings feelings of hopelessness, despair, and insecurity. This parent has been working on replacing this negative thought, which she has recognized she has quite often, with this more reasonable thought: "My daughter is in a lot of pain, but we are learning positive coping strategies to help her cope better."

There are three rules to follow for thought replacement to be effective:

1. You have to believe the reasonable or positive thought. This strategy doesn't work if you choose a thought that you don't believe, like "Everything is just fine," when it is not.
2. Catch yourself as much as you can when you have the negative thought so that you have lots of chances to try out your new positive thought. It takes practice, and you'll have to get good at monitoring yourself.
3. Let go of your negative thoughts. Thoughts are just thoughts. Negative thoughts don't usually lead to good problem-solving. It is okay to let a negative thought go away—it doesn't mean that you don't care about things or want to solve the problem. You can use better methods to do that, though.

Here are some examples of common negative thoughts and positive alternatives:

Negative Thought	Positive Thought
"My child's pain will never get better."	"We are doing everything we can to help her cope with the pain and get her back to her regular life."
"I am so tired, I don't know how much more of this I can handle."	"I have been through a lot in my life. I can get through this, too."
"Nothing we do is helping."	"My daughter has had pain for a long time and it can take just as long to get better. Lately, she is having more good days than bad days."

Positive Self-Statements

Everyone experiences negative and positive emotions. We know that negative emotions can lead to unproductive worries, negative self-judgment, and narrow attention that make it hard for a person to see the whole picture. Have you heard the expression, "She can't see the forest through the trees?" This refers to the difficulty in grasping the whole situation; something that happens when we have a lot of negative emotions. Alternatively, positive emotions can make approaching problems easier and more effective. One way of helping to stay positive is to use positive self-statements. Following is a list of positive self-statements that other parents have found helpful.

- I can solve this problem!
- I'm okay—feeling sad is normal under these circumstances.
- I can't direct the wind, but I can adjust the sails.
- I don't have to please everyone.
- I can replace my fears with faith.
- There will be an end to this difficulty.
- If I try, I can do it!
- I can get help from _____ if I need it.

- It's easier, once I get started.
- I deserve to relax.
- I can cope with this!
- I can reduce my fears.
- I just need to stay on track.
- I can manage this situation.
- I'm proud of myself!
- I can hang in there!

Thought STOPping

A third strategy for reducing negative thoughts is called thought STOPping and is another way to direct attention away from negative thoughts. There are three steps for effective thought STOPping (you can practice the steps later):

1. Think a negative thought to yourself. Now say "STOP" in a very loud voice (you might want to be alone the first time you practice this). It is important to say this out loud so that you have a good memory of what your voice sounds like. Each time you have that negative thought, shout "STOP"! Repeat this a few times.
2. Think a negative thought to yourself. Now try saying "STOP" to yourself in your mind instead of out loud. Try to imagine your voice as it was when you were saying "STOP" out loud. Practice this a few times.
3. Think a negative thought to yourself. Now picture a bright red stop sign in your head. Picture every detail, the big white letters, the white trim and the exact shade of red. Now when you have that thought say "STOP" to yourself and picture that red stop sign. Practice this a few times until your thought goes away.

Summary

In this chapter, we reviewed the important role that parents and caregivers play in modeling coping strategies for children with chronic pain. We discussed ways that you can model effective methods of coping with pain, stress, and other problems for your child. You learned several positive coping skills, including problem-solving steps, thought replacement, positive self-statements, and thought STOPping. These positive coping skills may help you to reduce your own stress, improve your mood, and reduce your anxiety. Modeling these positive coping skills for your child may help improve his or her ability to cope with pain, manage stress, and solve problems in his or her daily life.

Chapter 8   Practice Assignment

There are several ways that you can practice the skills discussed in this chapter.

1. If you or another adult in your household have a pain problem or experience something stressful, consider the coping strategies that are being shown to your child. Think about the helpful responses to pain and stress that you would like to see your child imitate. What things may be unhelpful that are being shown to your child or teen? Think about the unhelpful responses to pain and stress that you can reduce.

2. Identify one or two positive coping responses to stress or pain that you want to model for your child.

3. Find a time to talk with your child, however briefly, about how you solve a problem or cope with a stressful situation.

4. Try out the problem-solving steps with at least one problem. Go through each step, and at the end of a week, evaluate your progress. You can also teach the problem-solving steps to your child and other members of your family so that they can use these steps as well.

5. Monitor your own negative thoughts and try using thought replacement, positive self-statements, or thought STOPping to help reduce your own stress.

These are ways that I will model positive coping strategies for my child:

1. _____

   _____

2. _____

   _____

3. _____

   _____

These are positive coping skills that I will use to better solve problems, deal with negative thoughts, and reduce my own stress:

1. _____

_____

2. _____

_____

3. _____

_____

Special Topics by Age and Developmental Level: Issues for Young Children and Older Adolescents

Cooper is a 17-year-old with chronic migraines. He is struggling to get along with his parents. He wants to attend an out-of-state college next year. His parents are worried about what will happen to him if he has a severe migraine and is far away from home. Cooper feels like his parents will never let him grow up.

Susie is a 9-year-old with arthritis who has trouble falling asleep and staying asleep at night because of pain. Her mother spends several hours every night trying to help Susie fall asleep by singing to her, reading to her, and lying with her in bed. Once Susie does fall asleep, she is usually up within a few hours complaining of pain. Her mother is tired and wonders how much longer she can keep this up.

THIS CHAPTER COVERS SPECIAL TOPICS FOR YOUNG CHILDREN (under age 10) and older adolescents (over age 14). Although we use these two age groups as a guideline, the information provided in this chapter is important for all parents. We review strategies that may be useful to you now and as your child grows older.

Special Topics for Young Children

Parents of young children will learn here about managing their child's medications, encouraging positive coping skills, supporting physical activity, and limit setting.

Managing Medications

Young children rely on their parents to establish structure and a daily routine. Developmentally, young children do not yet have the cognitive skills needed to manage pain independently. These skills include planning, organization, and long-term memory. Because these skills are not fully developed, we expect parents to play a major role in helping their young children to manage pain.

For children under the age of 10 years, parents should be in charge of all medications and supplements. Medications and supplements should be stored in a secure location out of the child's reach. Parents should administer pain medication exactly as prescribed by their child's doctor.

Parents should administer pain medication exactly as prescribed by their child's doctor.

Parents of young children often struggle with when to give medications prescribed on an as-needed basis. Some children may verbally request pain medication when they are hurting, while others may appear to be in pain but never request medication. Still others may request pain medication more frequently than is prescribed or recommended. As a parent, you know your child best. If you are having a hard time determining when to give an as-needed medication to your child, we recommend that you speak with your child's doctor in order to come up with a plan that works for your family.

Some young children won't take prescribed medications for their pain problem because they don't like to swallow pills. This can also be a problem for adolescents who never learned to swallow pills. Learning to swallow pills is an important developmental task to accomplish because throughout life not all medications are readily available in liquid or chewable form. The good news is that it does not take long to teach children how to swallow pills. Here we have provided the same steps that psychologists use to teach children this important skill. The process is straightforward and we believe that all parents can follow it. As you work through these steps, it is important that you praise your child's efforts and her success (see Chapter 4 for a review of how to use praise). You will need small candies of different sizes (found in the cake decorating aisle of the supermarket) as well as Tic-Tacs.

STEP-BY-STEP PILL-SWALLOWING TRAINING

1. Make sure your child is capable of the swallowing reflex. Ask your child to swallow a mouthful of water from a cup. If there are no problems swallowing water, you can move on to the next step.
2. Your child should begin with the size candy that he or she can comfortably swallow. For some children, this may be the smallest possible candy, such as the very tiny multicolored round balls called mixed decors or tiny nonpareils. Tell your child to place one ball as far back on the tongue as possible, take a drink of water from a cup, and swallow the pill. Your child can have as many practice trials as needed. Most children find swallowing the tiny mixed decors surprisingly easy. Praise your child for both the effort and success.
3. After your child has successfully swallowed the candy five times you can move on to the next size. Practice trials should be given with each new size. You can use the following as a guide for the different sizes of pills:
   a. Tiny round mixed decors or nonpareils
   b. Jimmies or sprinkles
   c. Snowflake or flower decors
   d. ½ Cinnamon décor or nonpareil
   e. Whole cinnamon décor or nonpareil
   f. Tic-Tacs
4. If your child is unable to swallow a candy five times in a row, stay on this step. You should continue with the same size of candy even if your child has swallowed the pill successfully

four times in a row and failed on the fifth try. That being said, training sessions should last no more than 10–15 minutes. After that you can take a break and pick up where you left off on another day. Sessions can be even shorter than this depending on how well your child is tolerating the procedures. To decide when to end the session, consider the following:

    a. How much water your child has had to drink

    b. How much candy your child has eaten

    c. The extent to which your child appears anxious about the pill-swallowing training

5. If your child moves to the next size candy and is not successful, go back to the previous size before ending the session. It is important that your child end the session with success. Be sure to praise your child for his or her efforts at the end of the session.

6. In subsequent sessions, always begin with the largest size candy your child was able to swallow successfully. If your child swallows this easily on the first attempt, move on to the next size. If your child is not successful, move back to the previous size. Continue to offer as many practice trials as your child needs, using the criterion of five successful swallows in a row before moving on to the next size. Some children move through all the sizes in one session, while others may require multiple sessions.

7. Once your child masters Tic-Tacs, you can progress to the actual medication. Many children experience success with the actual medication once they have success with Tic-Tacs. If not, you can consider adding additional levels of larger-sized candies to gradually approximate the size of the medication.

Using Positive Coping Skills

Parents also play a critical role in helping young children to use positive coping skills. In Chapter 3 we described relaxation skills that you can teach to your child to help him or her manage the pain. In our experience, young children typically benefit most from abdominal breathing and progressive muscle relaxation. Guided imagery may also benefit young children. Young children need support from parents to practice positive coping skills. Support your young child in practicing these positive coping skills by helping him or her set up a regular time and place to practice. Practice these skills with your child at first, and then provide the child with opportunities to practice on his or her own. If your child is having trouble practicing these skills, consider using a reward system to increase motivation to practice (see Chapter 4).

Parents of young children often wonder how to respond to their child when he or she complains of pain. During a pain flare, young children often need reminders from parents to use positive coping skills. We recommend simply acknowledging that your child is not feeling well and talking to him or her about what he or she can do to manage the pain. You can ask your child, "What do you think you can try to help your pain?" You can encourage your child to try the positive coping strategies you have taught her (Chapter 3).

> During a pain flare, young children often need reminders from parents to use positive coping skills.

Limit Setting

At one point or another, all parents have difficulty setting limits with their children. For parents of young children with chronic pain, this can be particularly challenging. It may be hard to tell how much help their child needs from them to cope with pain. Going to sleep independently is one example of a behavior that can be challenging. As mentioned in Chapter 6, it is common for children with chronic pain to have difficulty falling asleep and staying asleep. For young children, this can mean that they are resistant to going to bed (e.g., stall, refuse to get in bed) or that when they wake in the middle of the night they come to their parents for assistance. It may be difficult to know how much help your child needs from you to fall asleep and stay asleep. Over time, the attention you give your child during the night can lead to more sleep difficulties for your child (and also for you!). You may be accidentally reinforcing your child's bedtime resistance and night wakings with the extra time you are spending with him or her at night.

Another example that many parents struggle with is time on electronics or screen time. It is common for young children with chronic pain to want to spend more time in front of screens and less time participating in sports or other physical activities. For many children, physical activity may make pain worse, while spending time in sedentary activities may provide some relief. In fact, many parents tell us that the only time their child does not complain of pain is when he or she is watching TV or playing a computer or video game. As a result, it can be very difficult to set limits on the amount of time children with chronic pain spend on screens. However, more screen time means there is less time available for physical activity. Over time, failing to set limits on your child's screen time can inadvertently lead to less physical activity, increased muscle weakness, and worse pain.

In general, it can be helpful to talk to your child about the methods that he or she can use to cope with pain that do not require your help or excessive use of screen time. For example, your child may be able to use heat (e.g., safely plug in a heating pad) or cold (e.g., take ice out of the freezer) on his or her own. Your child may be able to listen to audio files of relaxation exercises on a preloaded mp3 player. He or she may be successful at using deep breathing on his or her own, too. You can use prompts to encourage your child to use these strategies independently during the day and at night. One strategy that can be useful is to start with a high level of support at first (e.g., being there to show your child how to use relaxation during a pain flare), but then over time to gradually reduce your involvement so that your child is using these skills on his or her own. You can also consider making and implementing a reward system to support your child for practicing or attempting to use coping skills, reducing screen time, improving sleep habits, or attaining other goals (see Chapter 4). Sometimes parents make extra reward opportunities available to their children when they are observed using coping skills independently.

> Start with a high level of support at first, but then over time gradually reduce your involvement so that your child is using pain coping skills on his or her own.

Checking in About Pain

Young children may not use language to describe their pain that really helps their parents understand how they feel. You may worry that if you do not check in with your child about the pain that you will miss important information about his or her condition. You may also worry that your child will not know that you care about him or her if you do not ask your child how he or she is feeling. But asking children too often about how they are feeling can lead them to pay too much attention to the pain. In general, even for young children, we recommend that parents get rid of pain check-ins. That is, let your child come to you to ask for help with the pain rather than asking your child if he or she is okay. If you do notice that your child seems to be in pain (e.g., through the child's facial expression), encourage him or her to use the coping strategies you have learned in this book. You can also work on increasing age-appropriate communication about other topics, such as hobbies, friendships, and family activities.

Providing Opportunities for Physical Activity

As discussed in Chapter 5, maintaining physical activity is important for children with chronic pain. Young children may want to stop participating in activities for fear of hurting more or because they believe that having pain prevents them from doing anything physically active. Remember that young children think more concretely. You can encourage physical activity by setting up play dates, family outings, and organized sports. We recommend that all parents set an expectation that their child can participate in some activities. For young children, parents have complete control over the outside activities that their child participates in. Young children need their parents to take them to and from activities, so the choices need to fit into your family's schedule.

You can also model how to maintain a physically active lifestyle by participating in your own exercise routine and engaging in physical activity with your child. Young children will look to their parents for direction when they are afraid to participate in an activity because of pain. You can encourage your child to use positive coping strategies to help with participating in activities. You can also consider setting up a reward system to help motivate your child to participate in physical activity (see Chapter 4).

> We recommend that all parents set an expectation that their child participate in some physical activities.

Special Topics for Adolescents

Parents of older adolescents will learn skills here that can help them communicate with their teen, support teens in becoming independent, and address risky health behaviors such as smoking and alcohol use.

Communication

For parents, adolescence is often a challenging time filled with many changes in relationships, behaviors, activities, and interests. Parents and teenagers can have trouble communicating, for a number of reasons. Teens spend more time outside the home with friends, participating in extracurricular activities, or working at a job. This means they spend less time with family. As a result, parents have fewer opportunities to communicate with their teens, and in this limited time during which parents and teens see each other, parents often have to enforce rules and set limits. If the teen's wants and desires are at odds with what parents allow, conversations may become more confrontational. Teens are also often less interested than younger children in interacting with their parents. Many parents have a hard time starting conversations with their teens. Teens can be hard to pull information out of, and sometimes they are downright rude. Communication strategies that worked when your child was younger may not work anymore.

Pain can further change the way that parents and teens communicate. The ways in which you interact with your teen may be different now from when your teen had no pain problem. Often parents find that they have started communicating for their teen rather than letting the teen speak for him- or herself.

Communicating effectively with your teen is important. Good communication can lead to less stress for you and for your teen. It can also help your teen become more independent in managing pain. Communication skills are essential to implementing other strategies effectively (such as reward systems). That being said, effective communication is a two-way street. As a parent, you must be able to deliver a clear message that is understood by your teen. In return, you must be open to hearing what your teen has to say to you. Research shows that fewer conflicts arise in families where communication is better. Fewer conflicts can mean less stress for you and your teen.

COMMUNICATION BARRIERS

Communication barriers are habits that get in the way of effective communication. Most parents say and do things that get in the way of communicating with their teen at some point. Certain types of communication barriers are common among parents and teens; these are listed below, along with alternative ways of communicating that you can try. Think about whether any of these communication barriers apply to your family. You can practice ways of communicating that overcome these barriers. This can improve your ability to communicate with your teen.

Labeling and belittling: Teens may inadvertently get the message that you don't value them and their ideas when you say things like "What do you know? How many years have you had to deal with finances?" or "Your pain is never going to get better with that attitude."

Try instead: Start your statements with "I" instead of "You." For example: "I'm worried that your sad thoughts are making your pain worse."

Coddling and being overly helpful: Coddling and being overly helpful can make it hard for your teen to practice doing things on his or her own. Saying things like "Don't worry sweetie, I'll take out the trash for you" can make teens feel that they are not capable of doing these things and that you don't believe they are.

Try instead: Expect your teen to participate in normal activities even when in pain. When your teen complains of pain, encourage him or her to use coping strategies such as relaxation or distraction. When your teen participates in normal activities when in pain, give him or her specific, labeled praise. For example: "Thank you for taking the trash out even though you have a headache. I really appreciate it when you do your chores."

Giving orders: Teens are not likely to listen to orders like "Do the dishes now! You never do what I say."

Try instead: Talk to your teen about how you can work together to solve the problem. For example: "I feel frustrated when you don't help around the house. What can we do to make it easier for you to help with chores?"

Lecturing and giving unsolicited advice: Teenagers often are not open to hearing advice from their parents when they do not ask for it. Comments like "You need to get all A's on the rest of your assignments this quarter if you want to pass your classes" will make most teenagers either get angry or check out.

Try instead: Try simply stating the problem. For example: "I'm worried about how you are doing in school this semester."

Pleading and bribing: Pleading and bribing may have worked when your teen was younger, but are unlikely to work now. Saying things like *"Please,* you have got to go to school today. I'll give you *anything you want* if you go to school today" teaches your teen that he or she can get rewards if he or she waits until you get upset or are desperate before doing the desired behavior.

Try instead: Set reasonable expectations for your teen and stick to them. If your teen is having a hard time meeting your expectations, you can consider using a reward system (Chapter 4).

Mixed messages: Mixed messages occur when parents give encouragement and negative feedback at the same time. For example: "Great job on your math test! Why couldn't you have done this well on your other exams?" Another example is "Your room is looking much cleaner today! I don't know how your sister manages to keep her room clean *all the time.*" Mixed messages can decrease your teen's motivation to succeed. Mixed messages tell your teen that he or she is not good enough, no matter how hard he or she tries.

Try instead: Provide your teen with specific, labeled praise when your teen does something you want him or her to do. For example: "Great job on your math test! You worked really hard for that." Another example is "Thank you for cleaning your room even though you were not feeling well." You will learn more about praise later in this chapter.

Needing to get the last word: Many parents of older adolescents feel like they need to get the last word in during an argument, especially when they think their teen is making a mistake. In fact, this strategy will make your teen less likely to listen to you.

Try instead: Catch yourself when you are saying the same thing repeatedly to your teen. It can also be helpful to step back and just listen to your teen. You can also practice taking a few slow, deep breaths and being silent. Listening will let your teen know that you are interested in his or her feelings and opinions, even when you disagree.

CHARACTERISTICS OF EFFECTIVE COMMUNICATION

Characteristics of effective communication are listed below. You may already be using some of these strategies with your teen or other people in your life. Practicing these communication strategies can improve your ability to communicate with your teen.

Be direct. For example: "I am worried about your grades. You have missed a lot of school lately because of pain." Don't beat around the bush when approaching a topic, and be careful not to send indirect messages, such as, "I guess I'm going to have to talk to your teacher about your math test." Indirect messages often include subtle threats, which undermine communication.

Be assertive. Being assertive can help get people to listen to you. To make sure you have someone's attention, make eye contact with them, or touch them on the shoulder.

Include your perspective and feelings. Instead of saying "You never help around the house," try "I get really frustrated when you don't help around the house. I know you don't feel 100% all the time, but I could really use your help cleaning up." This statement allows your teen to see things from your point of view.

Listen carefully. You can't have two-way communication if you are the only one talking. Try taking turns talking to make sure you both have a chance to participate in the conversation. This may mean pausing, not interrupting, and creating silence (this can be uncomfortable for some parents) to give your teen a chance to think and speak about the topic.

Plan what you want to say before you say it. When broaching touchy subjects, don't jump into the conversation without thinking first about what you want to say. Try thinking about what you want to say before you bring up sensitive topics such as your teen's grades, his or her friends, or how pain is impacting his or her life.

One of the most important ways to get your teenager to listen to you is to *listen to him or her*. Talking is how teens figure things out. Let

One of the most important ways to get your teenager to listen to you is to listen to him or her. your teen know that you are willing to just listen. Practice paying attention to what he or she is saying, even when you don't like what is being said. Show interest in his or her feelings and opinions, even when you disagree. Practice sitting back and listening even when you have the urge to take over the conversation and tell him or her what you think is right. When you are listening to your teen, it is important to use questions sparingly. Resist the urge to know why your teen is thinking in a particular way. Giving your teen some privacy and space can help your teen to be more open in conversations with you.

When you are dealing with a conflict, express your feelings and needs directly. Giving a clear message may mean saying, "I worry when you don't check in with us after school," instead of "You never let us know where you are." Let your teen know how his or her behavior affects you. Avoid judging your teen as being good or bad.

We recommend that the adults in your family avoid talking about problems related to your teen's pain in front of him or her. Teens with chronic pain often feel like they are burdening their parents. Hearing parents discussing things like frustrations with doctors or financial problems can be very stressful for teens. Find a private time and place to discuss these issues and vent your frustrations without your teen being in earshot.

As we discuss later in this chapter, it is important to respect your teen's growing autonomy (independence). Instead of solving problems for your teen, try working together. For example, instead of nagging your teen to practice physical therapy exercises, work with your teen to come up with strategies that may make it easier for him or her to remember to practice on his or her own. Involving your teen in this process will make it more likely that the teen will follow through on the plan that you make.

Parents who enjoy effective communication with their teen make themselves available to talk to their teen at any time. They also learn to not be reactive to their teen's negative moods and irritability. Teens often blurt things out or want to talk at inconvenient times. Be open to listening to your teen anytime, anywhere, even if he or she is being cranky and unpleasant. If it really is an inconvenient time for you, set up a specific time to talk about the issue with your teen. For example, "What you're saying is important to me. I can tell you are upset about it. Let's discuss it after dinner." You can also learn to lessen your response to negativity and crankiness. Being calm and neutral will go much farther than trying to change your teen's bad mood or arguing with him or her about it.

Communicate directly with your teen to set limits and expectations. Let your teen know what your unbreakable rules are. At the same time, let your teen make an increasing number of minor decisions. For example, set clear expectations for behaviors that you want most to change (e.g., increasing school attendance, improving grades), and let your teen have a say in the rewards he or she will earn for meeting those expectations. You can revisit Chapter 4 for a review of skills to help you with this.

The following list summarizes strategies for establishing effective communication habits with your teen. You may be using many of these skills already. Think about which of these you want to practice with your teen.

- Sit back and listen, even when you have the urge to tell your teen what you think. Use questions sparingly.
- Express your feelings and needs directly.
- Do not talk about the impact of your teen's pain problem on your life in front of him or her. Discuss your feelings about medical providers, financial troubles, and job stress in private.
- Support your teen's growing independence by working with him or her to solve problems, instead of solving problems for your teen.
- Be open to listening to your teen anytime, anywhere.
- Increase your tolerance for your teen's bad moods and irritability. Learn to respond neutrally and calmly.
- Communicate directly to set limits and expectations.

KEEPING COMMUNICATION POSITIVE

What is the daily ratio of positive, encouraging words that you say to your teen, compared to the number of complaints, orders, criticisms, warnings, pleadings, lectures, and discouraging words? Research shows that parents spend very little time actually talking with teens (on average, less than 20 minutes a day). As a result, most parent-to- teen communication is used to register a complaint, give a command, or ask for assistance. This does not mean that all of this communication is negative—it may simply be necessary, like making car arrangements.

There are several strategies you can use for keeping communication positive:

1. Take time to relax and have fun. Teens need to learn positive ways to manage stress. Enjoying each other's company will build lifetime relationships. Establish a regular one-on-one time with your teen, such as one night per week that you cook dinner together, go to the mall together, or play a game together.

2. Have a weekly or biweekly family meeting where everyone can share what is going well at home and what they would like to change. This helps kids feel like their opinions matter. Get input from each person on rules and curfews as well as on the consequences of breaking rules. Make agreements, try them out; modify them as needed. In Chapter 7, you learned about problem-solving skills. You can teach this set of skills to your family and then use them to help solve family problems.

3. Give straightforward advice on topics such as sex, drinking, and drugs, but DON'T keep repeating it. Teens need to hear your opinions, but not over and over again.

4. Show physical affection. Teens are still kids. They need the warm feelings of belonging that come from good touches and hugs.

5. Give lots of praise and positive feedback. Teens need to hear the "good stuff" just like the rest of us. You will learn more about using praise later in this chapter.

6. Reduce general chaos, negativity, and arguing between all family members. Effective communication is more likely to happen when things are calm.

7. Keep a sense of humor. Teens often respond well to poking fun at yourself or the situation you are in.

The ratio of positive to negative communication is important. The higher the ratio of positive to negative, the closer you'll feel to your teen. When you have more positive communication with your teen, he or she will be more likely to listen to you. It is impossible to completely eliminate negative or necessary communication, so the best way to increase your ratio is to increase the positives.

How do other parents tackle parent-to-teen communication challenges?

"The two of us went to dinner and talked. I tried to listen and not interrupt too much so I could empathize with what he is going through. He was very open and we had a nice dialogue."

—Bryn, mother of a 12-year-old with functional abdominal pain

"We had a family meeting to discuss what has been going on with the negative speaking in the house from others and how we need to change this going forward. Elise was very receptive to the idea of speaking openly about what has been troubling her at school."

—Ellen, mother of a 16-year-old with chronic migraine

"I used 'I' instead of 'you' when talking with her. I also did my best to not interrupt when she was talking to me. When she wanted to spend time talking or being with me, I made the time, even if I was doing something else."

—Martin, father of a 14-year-old with complex regional pain syndrome (CRPS)

"I've practiced not giving orders and lecturing. It has relaxed some of the 'attitude' she has when she needs to be reminded to do her chores around the house."

—Jennifer, mother of a 17-year-old with fibromyalgia

"I sometimes tend to, as my husband calls it, 'beat a dead horse.' This week I made sure I didn't explain things to death. Instead, I was direct and then waited for a response from him. This worked really well."

—Leah, mother of a 15-year old with foot pain

INCREASING OPPORTUNITIES TO COMMUNICATE WITH YOUR TEEN

For teens with chronic pain, conversations with parents can become heavily focused on pain. Given the limited amount of time that most parents have to talk with their teens each day, it is important to increase opportunities to communicate with your teen and make topics other than pain a priority. Are there activities that you and your teen might like to do together? Hanging out with your teen gives him or her the chance to talk with you if he or she feels like it. Consider preparing a meal together, working on a craft project, playing a game, or going to the mall or to a sporting event. Increasing physical activity is an important part of treating your teen's pain and also a good way to spend time with your teen. Go for a walk or to the gym, or play a sport together.

Supporting Your Teen's Growing Independence

Adolescence is a time when teens gain increasing levels of independence and autonomy. This is a normal and healthy learning process. Common milestones of adolescence that mark increasing levels of independence include getting a driver's license, applying to college, having a romantic relationship, and securing a part-time job. Parents often spend time working with their teens to support them in achieving these goals.

"My son and I made dinner together this week so we could spend time doing something different. Our focus was on preparing dinner, so it was easier for him to communicate about how he was feeling since the focus wasn't on him entirely."

—Lindsay, mother of a 14-year-old with back pain

When your teen has chronic pain, however, supporting your teen in becoming independent can be difficult. Many parents have a hard time allowing teens with chronic pain to do developmentally normal "teenage things." For some parents, this can happen out of fear that certain activities may make pain worse or worries that their teen can't cope with the challenge. For example, parents may encourage their teen to delay applying for college out of concern that this may increase stress and make pain worse. Or, parents may discourage their teen from working at a part-time job out of concern that the teen won't be able to handle the physical demands. In other cases, the teen's pain problem may take up so much of the family's resources that other tasks of adolescence are pushed aside. For example, parents may prioritize taking their teen to medical appointments instead of scheduling driver's education classes.

Parents play an important role in their teens' development by encouraging age-appropriate independence in pain management and other activities of daily life. Adolescence is an ideal time for your teen to practice managing the responsibilities of his or her daily life. As you work on this with your teen, you can monitor progress and provide support as needed. Supporting your teen in working toward independence during adolescence will ensure that he or she will be able to meet these challenges in adulthood.

"I showed Alec how to renew prescriptions by phone. I am also teaching him how to contact the pain clinic to request new prescriptions when he runs out of refills."
—Marguerite, mother of a 16-year-old with fibromyalgia

There is a lot of variability in how teenagers navigate their way from being completely dependent on parents to being completely independent. Your teen may be more independent in some areas than others. Effective communication can help you to encourage your teen to become more independent.

Check out these common areas in which teens may need extra encouragement from parents to become independent. In some instances, your teen may be pushing you away in order to establish independence. In others, your teen may still need your help.

- **School**
  - Keeping track of assignment due dates
  - Making up missed schoolwork
  - Studying for exams
  - Planning appropriately for completing larger projects
  - Talking to teachers and other school staff about his or her pain problem
- **Friends**
  - Planning activities without help from parents
  - Managing conflicts with friends
  - Talking to friends about his or her pain problem
  - Keeping in touch with friends when out of school
  - Making decisions about drug and alcohol use

- **Home and Family**
  - Completing chores without reminders
  - Managing conflicts with siblings
  - Negotiating for increased access to privileges (e.g., later curfew)
  - Obtaining a driver's license
- **Self-Care**
  - Remembering to take medications
  - Remembering to refill medications
  - Scheduling doctor's appointments
  - Completing physical therapy exercises without reminders
  - Practicing pain coping skills without reminders
- **Romantic Relationships**
  - Making decisions about sexual behaviors
  - Balancing time spent with a romantic partner versus other commitments
- **Community Activities**
  - Participating in after-school sports and clubs
  - Balancing time spent in extracurricular activities with time spent on other commitments
  - Talking to people in the community about the pain problem (e.g., coach, church leaders, neighbors)

Here are a few things you can do to encourage your teen's independence:

- Decrease your communication with your teen about pain. Don't ask your teen if he or she is in pain (reduce check-ins about pain). Trust that your teen will come to you if there are substantial changes in the pain problem or if he or she needs help.
- Decrease your communication about your teen's pain in the teen's presence. If you are at a doctor's appointment, allow your teen to speak for him- or herself about how he or she is feeling and how things are going for your teen.
- Encourage interactions with other teens his or her age.
- Let your teen do things by him- or herself when possible.

- Let your teen have opportunities to make decisions; give him or her choices (e.g., "As a reward, would you like to earn X-Box time or a trip to the movies?").
- Give words of praise when your teen does things independently.
- Don't be too quick to rescue or console if your teen is anxious, scared, or in pain; give him or her the opportunity to cope by him- or herself or use relaxation strategies.

Set appropriate limits and be consistent with them. If you are using a reward system, make sure other adults in your home are on board with the plan.

Talking to Your Teen About Risky Health Behaviors

Health risk behaviors such as tobacco, alcohol, and drug use (e.g., marijuana) are often established in adolescence. Many children begin experimenting with these substances at age 11 or 12, and most adults who use them started these behaviors during their own adolescence. Youth with chronic pain may be especially vulnerable to the negative effects of tobacco and alcohol because of the role of stimulants and depressants on pain and pain medications. Research suggests that tobacco and alcohol use is associated with increased pain among people who have chronic pain problems. Marijuana use is often associated with decreased motivation, which can make it difficult to achieve the goals that are an important part of treating chronic pain (e.g., increasing physical activity and maintaining normal school attendance). On the other hand, some patients use medical marijuana to control pain and other symptoms. However, there is no research indicating that medical marijuana is safe or effective for managing pain in children and adolescents. Parents play an important role in helping teens make choices about using tobacco, alcohol, and other

"I'm working on allowing Andy to set his own schedule with respect to how and when he studies for exams. I've been allowing him his space and just offering him support when he needs it."
—Peter, father of a 15-year-old with abdominal pain

drugs. Parents also play an important role in helping teens understand the impact of medical marijuana on their lives.

An important way that you can influence your teen's health risk behaviors is to set a good example. Smoking, drinking, and drug use are most common among teens whose parents also smoke or use alcohol or other drugs. If you don't engage in these health risk behaviors, keep it up. If you do engage in these health risk behaviors, be mindful about how your teen sees you doing this. Don't leave cigarettes, alcohol, or drug paraphernalia where your teen can find them. Try to avoid smoking, drinking, and using drugs in front of your teen. You can also consider talking to your doctor about ways to quit.

Another important thing that you can do is proactively talk to your teen about tobacco, alcohol, and drug use. Have open communication about these topics. Don't wait until your teen starts to smoke or drink to talk to him or her about it. You can use the communication strategies that you learned from this chapter to talk to your teen about his or her thoughts and feelings on these health risk behaviors. Listen to what your teen has to say. Ask if any of your teen's friends smoke, drink, or use drugs. Ask your teen how he or she will handle a situation of being offered drugs or alcohol. Get to know your teen's friends and where they tend to hang out. Praise your teen for making good choices.

It is also important to talk to your teen about rules for tobacco, alcohol, and drug use, and to follow through on the consequences. You may think that your teen doesn't care about your opinion. In fact, teens are less likely to use these substances when parents set firm expectations about them. If your teen is already engaging in one or more of these health risk behaviors, talk to your teen about his or her thoughts and feelings on quitting. Your child's doctor may also be able to help you talk with your child about this issue.

Summary

In this chapter, you learned about special topics for young children (under age 10) and older adolescents (over age 14). We reviewed information about managing your child's medications, encouraging positive coping skills, supporting physical activity, and setting limits. This chapter also included skills that can help you communicate with your teen, and information on how to support your teen in becoming independent and how to talk to your teen about health risk behaviors. At every age, parents have an important role in supporting their children in managing pain and reaching their goals.

Chapter 9   Practice Assignment

For parents of younger children, consider whether your child could use your assistance in managing medications, using positive coping skills, and maintaining physical activity, school attendance, and other activities of daily living.

For parents of older adolescents, consider whether there are any positive communication strategies that you would like to use more frequently, and whether you and your teen are engaging in any negative patterns of communication that you would like to change. You can also implement two or three of the strategies outlined in this chapter to support your teen in becoming more independent. All parents should talk to their teens about alcohol, tobacco, and drug use; you can use the strategies outlined in this chapter to help you have this conversation.

List the strategies you want to try this week here:

1. _____

   _____

2. _____

   _____

3. _____

   _____

Reflection, Maintenance, and Prevention

Christine, a 14-year old girl who is a cancer survivor, is finishing up her eighth visit for cognitive-behavioral therapy. Christine and her parents state that the two skills that worked best for her are relaxation strategies and improving her sleep habits. Christine has less pain and has reached her biggest goal that she set: getting to school every day. In thinking about potential challenges in the months ahead, Christine's parents identify the transition to high school as a likely source of stress that they will need to manage using the CBT skills they have learned.

T HIS CHAPTER IS MEANT TO GIVE YOU THE OPPORTUNITY TO REFLECT on your progress and to consider how you will maintain the gains you have made. We hope that you have been successful in reaching some of your goals and that you have identified several strategies that work well for you and your family. If you have received benefit from one or two strategies then that is reason for celebration! Some of our patients have formally celebrated their achievements in managing their chronic pain (such as with a special

CBT requires effort and practice. Victories achieved should be recognized and celebrated.

dinner). CBT requires effort and practice. Victories achieved should be recognized and celebrated. Your family may enjoy planning a special celebration to recognize the hard work put forth.

Having read this book, you have learned several cognitive-behavioral treatment strategies, and it is important to consider what you have achieved so far and how you will sustain the gains made. It is also important to identify the areas in which you may still have work to do. There may be some areas in which you and your child continue to experience difficulties; this is typical and to be expected. The process of planning ways to prevent relapses from occurring or reducing negative consequences when problems do arise again is referred to as "relapse prevention."

> To relapse means that you have a setback, take a turn for the worse, or slip back into old problems.

In this chapter we will review and help you evaluate the success of the various treatment strategies that you have learned from this book. We will also help you identify future high-risk situations that could create challenges for your child and family. Specifically, we will help you learn to celebrate your and your child's successes, identify remaining challenges, put together your coping strategy "toolbox," and make plans for dealing with possible future problems.

Successes

It is important to take stock of your successes and of your child's successes. We hope you have learned a lot of different strategies for helping your child cope with chronic pain. Now is a good time to review which strategies were effective.

Making Progress with CBT Skills

"CBT taught me how to cope with my daughter's chronic pain. It also taught her what to do with her pain. It gave us the tools to make it through the day. She began to function, and I learned how to divert her pain. We also learned that a schedule is very important, going to bed at the same time, getting up at the same time, and doing the chores even if she was in pain. The strategies also gave us ideas, such as finding a comfortable chair for school, explaining and working with the school about her pain, and giving her the opportunity to move around at school when she needed to. I learned to not baby my daughter, to not question her and to not dwell on the pain. She did much better if she had diversions. She needed to learn how to cope and take charge of her own being. Life would pass her by if she did not participate. This gave us the tools we needed."

—*Donna, mother of 15-year-old Bailey with chronic back pain*

It is common for parents to notice that after learning cognitive-behavioral strategies they become more aware of how they are reacting to their child's chronic pain condition. Parents may have recognized certain behaviors that were "adopted" by their child or by themselves that were counterproductive.

What two or three strategies do you believe worked best for you and your child? Try having a conversation with your child about this to get input on what he or she thinks worked well. These are the strategies that should have a permanent place in your toolbox (we'll get to the toolbox a little later) for use now and in the future.

Write the two or three strategies that worked best for you and your child:

1. _____

2. _____

3. _____

This is also a good time to reflect on whether you have reached the short-term goals you set for yourself and your child in Chapter 2. If you can find the goals you wrote down when you

"The pain episodes have become much less frequent since I started using the cognitive-behavioral skills. We both realize how much of a role stress plays in bringing on her pain. The relaxation techniques have helped a lot."
—*Salem, mother of a 17-year-old with headaches*

first started this book, pull them out and evaluate the progress you have made toward them. Many families are encouraged to see that progress has been made toward goals of, for example, increasing physical activity, improving sleep, getting to school more often, and having a more positive outlook. However, different circumstances and challenges exist for different families, so it is also normal for there to be goals that you have not yet reached or that you have only partially achieved.

Remaining Challenges

"He's been really good about dealing with pain on his own at school, but he forgets to take care of himself when he is with his friends," says Trudy, mother of a 12-year-old boy with chronic migraines. While you have probably been very successful in some areas, there may be other changes you would like to see that are more difficult or that simply take longer. Just as it is important to reflect on your successes, it is also helpful to understand remaining challenges. Think about the two or three things you would still like to work on and the remaining unmet goals you have for your child.

Reasons for Difficulties

There are several common reasons why setbacks happen or why children continue to experience difficulties. Some parents and children continue to worry that an underlying cause for the pain has not been found. As we mentioned before, this "waiting" can make it difficult to take action. In addition, having a high level of worry may interfere with trying new skills that could help your child manage pain and improve participation in important and fulfilling activities.

Sometimes families find that a new skill or strategy is not helpful the first time they try it, so parents and children may give up on that strategy. Keep in mind that it may take a few attempts before you see the benefits of a new strategy. In this case, there simply may not have been enough time or practice opportunities to determine whether the strategy is effective or whether changes will occur. It can also be difficult for parents to make time to try new cognitive and behavioral skills when they are balancing other demands related to work, raising other children, and managing a household. As one father whose daughter has complex regional pain syndrome admitted to us, "She was using relaxation strategies, but I'm not sure if she is any more." A strategy such as a reward plan may have been attempted, but parents end up having difficulty figuring out how to keep it going. It is hard to find the time and energy to keep a strategy in place for several weeks or months.

Children and teens can also have trouble trying new skills. Some may have negative thoughts about the cognitive-behavioral skills, such as the notion that certain skills are just too hard to do or simply expecting that they won't be helpful. Other times, life just seems to get in the way of learning new skills. For example, the illness of a grandmother or the loss of a relationship with a close friend or romantic partner can be upsetting and take attention away from learning the skills needed to manage pain.

As you can see, difficulties in trying and succeeding at new cognitive and behavioral pain management skills are common for parents and children. It can be helpful to consider whether the barriers you encountered trying a new skill earlier on still exist, or if there might be an opportunity to try these skills again now or in the future. Parents have often told us that a new strategy was much more successful months after the first time they tried it, so try not to give up on certain strategies after only one attempt. Often there is success to be had in implementing skills at these later times, when proper energy and attention can be put into your efforts. You can re-read this book in the future and try some of the skills again.

"My daughter's pain seemed to be getting better, but she's had some setbacks that have been very upsetting and disheartening. We are trying to get her back on track to have some hope and to not fall into the habit of 'I can't' do anything." —Jacquie, mother of 12-year-old with chronic jaw pain

Your Strategy Toolbox

You have learned a range of cognitive-behavioral strategies over the past several months. These strategies represent your "tools," and you may want to continue to use these tools if you need them in the future. A well-equipped toolbox can assist you when difficulties arise or in continuing to work on making changes now. It is helpful to evaluate the success of the various strategies you have learned and tried to implement.

From this book you learned about the following strategies. Read the list below and put a check mark next to the strategies from which either you or your child received some benefit.

How Pain Affects Children and Families (Chapter 1)
- ☐ Maintaining family routines
- ☐ Getting support from others
- ☐ Taking care of yourself

Getting Help and Setting Goals (Chapter 2)
- ☐ Scheduling regular check-in visits with your child's pediatrician
- ☐ Making specific achievable goals

Relaxation Methods for Children and Teenagers (Chapter 3)
- ☐ Deep breathing
- ☐ Progressive muscle relaxation
- ☐ Guided imagery
- ☐ Mini-relaxation

Praise, Attention, and Reward Systems (Chapter 4)
- ☐ Staying positive
- ☐ Using attention and praise to increase your child's positive coping behaviors
- ☐ Setting up a reward system to increase your child's participation in important daily activities

Lifestyle Factors (Chapter 5)
- ☐ Increasing uptime
- ☐ Scheduling pleasant activities
- ☐ Activity pacing

☐ Using positive language to communicate expectations about physical activity

☐ Making healthy eating and drinking habits

Sleep Interventions (Chapter 6)

☐ Improving sleep habits

☐ Using extinction (planned parent ignoring) to address bedtime resistance

☐ Using sleep restriction, sleep training, and relaxation skills to address trouble falling and staying asleep (insomnia)

School and Social Life (Chapter 7)

☐ Making a school plan to help your child reach school goals

☐ Working with school staff to support your child in reaching school goals

☐ Supporting your child's friendships

Coping with Pain, Stress, and Other Problems (Chapter 8)

☐ Modeling positive coping skills

☐ Using problem-solving steps to solve important problems

☐ Using positive thinking skills: positive self-statements, thought replacement, or thought STOPing

Special Topics by Age and Developmental Level: Issues for Young Children and Older Adolescents (Chapter 9)

☐ Focusing on special skills for younger children: managing medications, pill-swallowing training, limit setting, reducing pain check-ins, providing opportunities for physical activity

☐ Focusing on special skills for older adolescents: improving communication, supporting independence, talking about risky health behaviors

☐ Others: _____

Anticipating Challenges

"She has taken on a huge time commitment away from home by joining the school musical. She is excited but I think this will definitely add to her stress levels," says Sarah, mother of a 16-year-old with chronic back pain. Another component of relapse prevention is anticipation of future challenges and making plans for dealing with them. Anticipating future problems can be helpful because when we imagine ourselves successfully solving these problems we are more likely to be able to solve them when they do happen.

Think about your answers to the following questions, and write them down if you'd like:

- What is the biggest day-to-day challenge you expect to face with your child?

  _____

  _____

  _____

- What tool (from your toolbox) could be helpful in coping with this?

  _____

  _____

  _____

- What is the biggest challenge you are likely to face in the next month or two?

  _____

  _____

  _____

- What tool (from your toolbox) could be helpful in coping with this?

  _____

  _____

  _____

Changes in schedules and routines often present challenges for children and teens with chronic pain. They may have difficulty implementing strategies that were working well before the change in schedule. Some children just seem to lose motivation to use a coping skill once they are under more stress. Following are a few troubleshooting tips that can be helpful in addressing these challenges.

"It will be very difficult to stay on schedule once school is out for the summer."
—Chine, father of a 10-year-old with chronic widespread muscle pain

1. **Identify thought barriers**. Amanda had a headache and wanted to stay home from work. She thought to herself, "I just can't get out of bed." Negative thoughts can keep you from learning and using helpful tools. Amanda tried thinking about going to work as something positive that might ultimately help her daughter, because then her daughter would have a positive model for coping with pain. This helped her to be willing to try going to work.

2. **Be flexible when using strategies you've learned**. When the reward chart helped Carlos begin riding his bike regularly again, his dad worked with him to set up a less structured reward system for gradually getting involved in baseball. Carlos' dad agreed to take him and a friend to a movie on weekends when he had gone to practice three times during the week.

3. **Remember the importance of stress**. When Case's family moved across town, his mom remembered to prompt him to use his relaxation skills more often because she knew the move and change in routine would be hard for him.

4. **Be patient and stick with it**. Change can take time and may happen gradually. You may be doing everything properly in implementing new coping skills. Sometimes it just takes more time to see the benefits. You can continue to practice your new skills over the upcoming months and continue to see changes occur.

5. **When challenges arise, remember that you have multiple tools you can try**. Look at the list of tools that you checked off as part of your toolbox earlier in this chapter. These are all

strategies and skills you have learned from this book and that you felt were helpful for either you or your child. Remember that you can try out any of these strategies at any time.

6. **Practice effective communication with your child**. You can go back to Chapter 9 for a refresher on ways to reduce communication barriers and increase positive communication. In any situation where you feel there is a challenge or stressor, having more effective communication will almost always be helpful.

7. **Don't forget to take care of yourself**. Parents who have taken care of their own stress, anxiety, and worries can better help their child cope with pain. The problem-solving and positive thinking skills in Chapter 8 can help you reduce your stress and anxiety. In addition, using deep breathing and other relaxation skills can provide you with positive ways to regulate your own emotions and decrease pain and stress.

Take opportunities to continue working toward the short-term goals that you set for your child's pain management. You can also develop new goals over the coming weeks and months so that you continue to make progress toward where you want your child and family to be in the long term. Many children continue to make significant improvements for some time. We encourage you to review these chapters whenever you need a "refresher course" on the strategies you are working on.

Putting Together Your Toolbox

Your toolbox should contain the behavioral, communication, pain management, and lifestyle skills that you have learned from this book. Continue to use these strategies when you need them. Here is a brief summary of the major skills.

- **Taking care of yourself**: Children with chronic pain have more pain and more trouble participating in activities when their parents have more stress, anxiety, and negative feelings. When you take care of yourself, you are also taking care of your child. It is okay to lean on others for support during this challenging time. You can also use the relaxation skills (Chapter 3), problem-solving skills (Chapter 8), and positive thinking skills (Chapter 8) from this book to help reduce your stress and negative feelings.

- **Targeting behaviors to increase**: Think about the behaviors you would like to see your child show more of. You may want your child to spend more time practicing relaxation and positive thinking skills, or attend school more often, or help more around the house. Identifying these behaviors will help you figure out how to use other strategies such as reward plans to reach these goals.

- **Using attention and praise**: When your child's behavior leads to satisfying or rewarding consequences, he or she is more likely to do this behavior again. Paying attention to a child when he or she exhibits desirable behaviors will encourage more of this particular behavior.

- **Setting up a reward system**: You can use a point system or a privilege system to reward your child for engaging in behaviors you want to increase. You can use a copy of the point system and the privilege system presented in Appendices E and F.

- **Encouraging your child to use positive coping skills**: You can provide praise and rewards when you see your child using positive coping skills such as relaxation methods. You can also model positive coping skills for your child when you have a stressful or painful experience.

- **Making a school plan**: Talk to your child about his or her school goals. Work together to identify positive coping skills that he or she can use to help reach those goals. Meet with school staff to determine what the school can do to help your child be more comfortable in school and to make academic progress. See Chapter 7 for more information on school plans.

- **Getting other adults or school personnel to help**: Make sure other adults in your home and at school are aware of your child's reward plan and/or school plan. These other adults can help support and reinforce the plan.

- **Modeling coping skills**: Speaking your thoughts aloud can be effective for teaching your child about how you cope with problems, stress, or pain. As you speak, you show your child how to think through a particular problem or situation.

- **Modeling exercise or other healthy habits**: Think of ways that your whole family can have healthy exercise and nutritional

habits. You can take a walk as a family after a meal. You can
have a set time for breakfast, lunch, and dinner, and serve
healthy foods. You can send your child to school with a full
water bottle. You can help your child avoid caffeinated beverages.

- **Improving your child's sleep habits**: Remember the eight
  sleep tips:
  1. Have your child go to bed and wake up at the same time
     each day
  2. No weekend catch up sleep
  3. Limit naps
  4. Pay attention to healthy lifestyle habits
  5. Use beds only for sleeping
  6. Develop relaxing bedtime routines
  7. Minimize electronics in the bedroom and at bedtime
  8. Schedule adequate sleep for your child's needs

You can also use strategies from Chapter 6 to address specific
problems with falling asleep or staying asleep.

- **Improving your own sleep habits**: Parents may also benefit
  from developing good sleep habits to improve on their own
  sleep quality. You can use similar strategies if you are having
  problems with falling asleep or staying asleep.
- **Providing opportunities and reinforcement for physical activity**: Talk with your child about the types of physical
  activities he or she might be interested in doing. For some
  families, it can be easier to incorporate physical activity into a
  child's daily routine if it is structured as a formal class, lesson,
  or practice. And for children who don't have any preferred
  activities that are physically vigorous, be creative and find any
  type of pleasant activity that gets your child up and moving
  (e.g., shopping). You can also set limits on screen time; this
  will reduce excessive sedentary behavior (e.g., sitting on the
  couch playing video games).
- **Communication skills**: You can work on reducing communication that falls into these categories:
  1. Labeling and belittling
  2. Coddling and being overly helpful
  3. Giving orders

4. Lecturing and giving unsolicited advice
5. Pleading and bribing
6. Mixed messages

- **Problem-solving steps**: Use the six problem-solving steps to help find solutions to problems that are creating stress for you or your family. After you have mastered these skills, you can teach your child or other family members the same steps so that they can also learn to effectively solve problems.
- **Changing negative thoughts**: You learned three strategies for changing negative thoughts:
  1. Replacing negative thoughts
  2. Positive self-statements
  3. Thought STOPping

These strategies may help to reduce your own stress and anxiety and improve your mood.

- **Supporting your child's independence with pain management**: You learned ways to support your child in increasing his or her ability to talk about and manage pain. You can eliminate "check-ins" and instead let your child come to you to tell you how he or she feels and if your help is needed. You can praise and encourage your child to use positive coping strategies to manage pain him- or herself.

Summary

In this chapter, we reviewed the importance of reflecting on the progress you and your child have made since you started using the methods in this book. We reviewed all of the skills and urged you to identify the ones that have been most effective for you and your child. We also discussed the importance of considering difficulties you may have faced in implementing the skills. It is also important to consider whether you can overcome any of those barriers so that you can try those skills in the future. Finally, we

Your commitment to your child's health and well-being is vitally important to helping him or her reach important life goals.

discussed making plans for the future in terms of anticipating challenges you may face in the coming weeks or months and identifying the skills in your toolbox that may be helpful for dealing with those challenges.

We recognize the tremendous efforts that parents make to learn cognitive-behavioral skills and to implement them at home. Dealing with chronic pain takes an enormous amount of time, energy, and dedication. Your commitment to your child's health and well-being is vitally important to helping him or her reach important life goals. We hope you now feel better equipped to continue to work with your child to reach these goals.

Chapter 10 Practice Assignment

Your final assignment is to reflect on the progress you and your child have made since you started using the methods in this book. Think back on the goals you identified when you started the book and consider where you are now. Take opportunities to celebrate your successes, to continue working toward these goals, and to develop new goals over the coming weeks and months.

Appendices

- Appendix A. Instructions for Progressive Muscle Relaxation (for Young Children, Ages 5–9)
- Appendix B. Instructions for Progressive Muscle Relaxation (for Older Children, over Age 10)
- Appendix C. Instructions for Muscle Relaxation with Imagery
- Appendix D. Instructions for Mini-Relaxation
- Appendix E. Point System Worksheet
- Appendix F. Privilege System Worksheet
- Appendix G. Brainstorming Solutions Worksheet

Appendix A

Instructions for Progressive Muscle Relaxation (for Young Children, Ages 5–9)

(Reprinted with permission from Palermo, T. M. (2012). *Cognitive-Behavioral Therapy for Chronic Pain in Children and Adolescents.* New York: Oxford University Press.)

This is an exercise that will help you relax. It involves tensing your muscles and then relaxing them. We are going to go through your muscles, one by one, to relax them.

To get started, you should get comfortable by sitting in a chair, or lying down. Close your eyes, and relax. Take nice, deep breaths in . . . and let it out slowly. Take nice, easy breaths . . . not too fast, or too slow . . . whatever is comfortable for you . . . notice that your body is starting to feel relaxed and calm . . . when you breathe out, feel your body become heavy and relaxed. . . .

Pretend you have two lemons in your hands and you want to make lemonade. Take your hands and make tight fists, like you are going to squeeze the juice out of the lemons. Feel the tightness in your hand and arm as you squeeze. Now drop the lemon and relax.

Let's try it one more time. Okay, now drop the lemon. Notice how your muscles feel when they are relaxed.

Continue to breathe, but think about your arms. Pretend that you are a furry, lazy cat stretching its arms. Stretch your arms as far as they will go . . . that's good . . . now relax them. Let's do that again. . . . Now, notice that your arms feel heavy and relaxed. Let them hang loosely on your lap.

Now think about your shoulders and your neck. Let's pretend now that you're a turtle . . . tuck your head into your shell, just like a turtle . . . good . . . now, take a deep breath and relax your shoulders and neck. Notice how good it feels to have relaxed muscles.

Now focus on your jaw muscles . . . bite down as hard as you can, just like you would bite down on a big jawbreaker . . . hold it . . . good, now relax your jaw.

Now, pretend that there is pesky fly on your nose, then on your forehead. You have to scrunch your face to get it off . . . hold it . . . good, now relax your whole face.

Now think about your stomach . . . pretend that an elephant is about to step on your belly. Then, make your belly as skinny as you can . . . so skinny you can squeeze through a fence . . . hold it . . . good, now relax your belly. Notice how good it feels to have relaxed muscles . . . now think about your legs and feet. Pretend that you're on a beach, and you have your toes in the warm sand. Stick your toes deep in the sand . . . as far as they can go . . . good, now relax your toes. Notice how relaxed your whole body feels after all the tightening and relaxing of muscles.

Appendix B

Instructions for Progressive Muscle Relaxation (for Older Children, over Age 10)

(Reprinted with permission from Palermo, T. M. (2012). *Cognitive-Behavioral Therapy for Chronic Pain in Children and Adolescents.* New York: Oxford University Press.)

This is an exercise called progressive muscle relaxation. It involves tensing muscles and muscle groups for about 5 to 7 seconds and then relaxing them for 20 to 30 seconds. We will go through four different major muscle groups, including hands, forearms, and biceps; then your head, face, throat, and shoulders; then your chest, stomach, and lower back; and last your thighs, calves, and feet. To get started with this exercise, you should be comfortable either sitting in a chair with your head supported or lying down.

Get yourself as comfortable as you can, you can let your eyes close if you want to, and just think about paying attention to my voice. As your body becomes comfortable start thinking about how you are breathing. It is all you should think about—shut everything else out of your mind. If your attention does start to wander, that's okay, just bring your attention back to my voice. Now take a nice deep breath in filling up your stomach . . . and let it out slowly . . . focus all of your energy on thinking about each breath you take . . . let each breath fill your stomach slowly . . . and let it out slowly . . . good . . . take nice easy stomach breaths . . . not too fast or too slow, just whatever is comfortable for you . . . now begin to notice how with each breath, the body starts to feel relaxed and calm . . . with each breath out, feel your whole body become more heavy and relaxed.

Now as you continue to breathe in and out slowly, pay attention to your left wrist . . . clench your left fist, making it tighter and tighter . . . tighter . . . hold it (1,2,3,4,5,6,7) . . . now relax . . . notice the difference between a tight muscle and a loose one . . . notice how good it can feel to have all the tightness out of your hand and to feel a bit more heavy and relaxed. Now pay attention to your right wrist . . . clench your right fist, making it tighter and tighter . . . tighter . . . good, hold it (1,2,3,4,5,6,7) . . . now relax and let your fingers spread out . . . notice the difference between a tight muscle and a loose one . . . feel the tension leave your hands.

Now focus on your elbows and tense your biceps . . . pull your arms and fingers up toward your shoulders, both arms together . . . tense them as much as you can and notice the feelings of tightness . . . hold it (1,2,3,4,5,6,7) . . . now relax and straighten out both of your arms . . . let them hang loosely on your lap . . . let the relaxation flow all the way down your arms toward your fingers . . . notice how good this feels to let the tension out of your muscles.

Now focus on your shoulders and shrug them up toward your ears . . . and hold it (1,2,3,4,5,6,7) . . . now take a deep breath and let your shoulders relax and come back down into their natural position . . . and notice the difference between tension as your head was hunched up between your shoulders and now the relaxation spreading through your neck, throat, and shoulders . . . Now shrug your shoulders one more time all the way up toward your ears . . . keep the tension as you hunch your head down between your shoulders . . . go ahead and hold it (1,2,3,4,5,6,7) . . . now relax and feel the relaxation spreading through your neck, throat, and shoulders . . . enjoy how loose and easy your neck can feel as it balances on your relaxed shoulders.

Now pay attention to the muscles in your forehead . . . and focus on wrinkling your forehead and brow . . . bringing your eyebrows down and curling up your forehead and brow . . . holding it (1,2,3,4,5,6,7) . . . good . . . and now relax, smooth out your forehead . . . let yourself imagine your forehead is smooth, relaxed, and free of tension . . . Now focus on your head and wrinkle your forehead again as tight as your can . . . hold it (1,2,3,4,5,6,7) . . . and now relax, smooth it . . . let yourself imagine your entire forehead is smooth and relaxed . . . notice the good calm feeling of having relaxed muscles.

Now close your eyes as tightly as comfortable . . . hold it (1,2,3,4,5,6,7) . . . and now open your eyes and let them stay gently open . . . noticing the relaxation across your forehead and through your eyes . . . now focus on your jaw . . . clench your jaw by biting your teeth together hard and notice the tension in your jaw . . . hold it (1,2,3,4,5,6,7) . . . good, now relax . . . really feel the difference between tense muscles and relaxed muscles in your jaw right now . . . now press your lips together hard and notice the tension in your face . . . hold it (1,2,3,4,5,6,7) . . . now relax and let your mouth be comfortable and relaxed . . . notice the difference as your face becomes more relaxed and loose.

Now put your head back so that you are looking up toward the ceiling, you should feel tension in the muscles in the front of your neck . . . hold it (1,2,3,4,5,6,7) . . . and now relax, put your head back in its normal position and feel the difference as your neck muscles become more loose . . . Now put your head forward so that your chin is just about touching your chest . . . hold the position, tensing up the muscles in the back of your neck (1,2,3,4,5,6,7) . . . good, now relax and put your head back in its upright position and notice your neck muscles becoming more loose and more relaxed.

Now concentrate on your back—arch it slightly, making sure not to strain . . . focus on the tension in your lower back . . . hold it (1,2,3,4,5,6,7) . . . and then relax and focus on letting go of all the tension in the muscles of your lower back . . . notice how loose the muscles in your back can feel . . . Repeat that one more time . . . concentrate on your back—arch it slightly, focusing on the tension in your lower back . . . hold this position (1,2,3,4,5,6,7) . . . and then relax, let go of all the tension in the muscles of your lower back . . . feeling the looseness, enjoying the feeling of relaxation.

Now take a deep breath and hold it, notice the feeling of tightness in the chest (1,2,3,4,5,6,7) . . . then release the breath, and notice your chest muscles loosening, becoming more relaxed and more comfortable. Now focus on stomach muscles, make them tight by pulling your stomach inward into a ball . . . hold it (1,2,3,4,5,6,7) . . . and then relax, let your stomach muscles loosen, becoming more comfortable and free of tension.

Now curl your toes downward, making your calves tense, holding that position (1,2,3,4,5,6,7). . . . and now relax let your toes come back up and enjoy the feeling of relaxation in your calves . . . notice your leg muscles feel more loose and less tense. Now bend your toes upward toward your face and create tension in your shins . . . hold it (1,2,3,4,5,6,7) . . . now relax, let your toes back down and enjoy the feeling of heaviness and relaxation spreading throughout your legs. Now point your toes again toward your face and create tension in your shins and calves . . . hold it (1,2,3,4,5,6,7) . . . and relax . . . enjoy the feeling of relaxation throughout your legs and calves.

Feel the heaviness in your entire body now . . . enjoy the feeling of relaxation . . . enjoy how good this feels . . . when your whole body feels loose and calm . . . and it feels good to be in control of your body . . . if there are any muscles in your body that still feel tense, you can concentrate on that muscle group now and focus on relaxing that particular muscle group.

Appendix C

Instructions for Muscle Relaxation with Imagery

(Reprinted with Permission from Palermo, T. M. (2012). *Cognitive-Behavioral Therapy for Chronic Pain in Children and Adolescents.* New York: Oxford University Press.)

This is an exercise called muscle relaxation with imagery. It involves focusing on muscle groups while picturing a pleasant, relaxing image.

Lots of people really enjoy a hot tub or a hot bath as a way of getting relaxed. You can practice muscle relaxation by imagining or pretending that you are in a hot tub or a hot bath, and will use this as an example. You can also imagine a different relaxing place later on when you practice on your own.

To start, get a good picture in your head of a hot tub, hot bath, or warm pool . . . really clearly like you are watching it on T.V. You can picture yourself sitting on the side getting ready to get in the water. As you listen to this practice exercise, shut everything else out of your mind. If your attention does start to wander, that's okay, just bring your attention back to my voice.

Now take a nice deep breath in through your nose . . . and let it out slowly through puckered lips . . . let each breath fill your stomach slowly . . . and let your stomach down slowly . . . good . . . take nice easy breaths . . . not too fast or too slow, just whatever is comfortable for you . . . now begin to notice how with each breath, the body starts to feel relaxed and calm . . . with each breath out, feel your whole body become more heavy and relaxed.

As you look at the hot tub, you might like to feel the water first to get yourself used to it. You can sit on the side of the tub, placing the tips of your toes in the warm water and feel the warmth—how nice and good it feels. Then, slowly you can place your entire foot in the water, first your right foot and then your left. Notice how good it can feel to have the warm water circling around your feet.

Then you can go farther into the tub by stepping in lower so that your calves are now covered with the warm water. Relax . . . enjoy the feeling of relaxation throughout your legs and calves.

You can step in even deeper and focus on the feeling of warmth all over your legs, down your calves, and into your feet. Notice how good the warm water feels on your legs . . . you can enjoy having your legs feel a bit heavier and relaxed.

As you sit deeper in the hot tub, the water is now swirling around your stomach and lower back. You can feel the warmth all over your stomach, back, and legs. Relax . . . feel the looseness and enjoy the feeling of relaxation.

Now you may be ready to place your hands in the water, feeling the warmth of the water and then letting your hands hang loosely on your lap . . . let the relaxation flow all the way down your arms toward your fingers . . . notice how good this feels to let the tension out of your muscles.

If you like the feel of water jets, you can imagine that they have come on and are pushing the water toward you in a comfortable way. You may hear the rhythm of the jets as they pulse the water around the tub and help you feel more relaxed.

When you are ready, you can slide farther into the tub, feeling the warm water rise up to your chest and cover your hands and arms . . . enjoy the heaviness in your body and feeling your muscles relax.

Now you may like to feel the warmth of the water circling around your shoulder and neck muscles. Relax and feel the water circle around your neck and shoulders . . . enjoy how loose and easy your neck can feel in the warm water as it balances on your relaxed shoulders.

You may place your head gently backward now onto a soft cushion and feel the warm water around the base of your head. . . . let yourself imagine the warmth spreading through your entire face. Your face is getting smooth and relaxed . . . notice the good calm feeling of having relaxed muscles in your face.

Enjoy the feel of the warm water all over your body, relaxing your muscles and creating a sense of calm. Feel the heaviness in your entire body now . . . enjoy the feeling of relaxation . . . enjoy how good this feels . . . when your whole body feels loose and calm . . . and it feels good to be in control of your body.

Enjoy this feeling for a few more moments. When you're ready to finish, just move around a bit and stretch. You may feel relaxed and energized and ready to go back to your regular activity.

Appendix D

Instructions for Mini-Relaxation

(Reprinted with permission from Palermo, T. M. (2012). *Cognitive-Behavioral Therapy for Chronic Pain in Children and Adolescents.* New York: Oxford University Press.)

You can learn short methods to remind your body to relax throughout the day. This is a one-minute relaxation method that we call mini-relaxation.

To start, take a big, deep breath in through your nose, counting to 8 filling your stomach.

Hold it for a few seconds.

Now, breathe out through puckered lips, letting your stomach down slowly, and imagine all the tension in your body and mind leaving on this breath.

Choose a word or phrase that you say to yourself (such as "relax" or "calm") to let your body know to relax.

Check your body to see if there is any tension, especially in places where you know you often get tense.

Take another big, deep breath in through your nose, counting to 8 filling your stomach.

Hold it for a few seconds and say your relaxing word to yourself.

Now, breathe out through puckered lips, letting your stomach down slowly, and imagine that you can direct the breath to the tense spot.

As you breathe out, feel the tension go.

Take a few more breaths like this.

Breathe in . . . pause . . . out.

In . . . pause . . . out.

Feel the tension go.

Practice this mini-relaxation a few times each day so your body can get used to relaxing any time that you need to.

Appendix E

Point System Worksheet

Week of: ___/___/____

Activities to Reward

_____ will receive points for the following activities. He or she is responsible for tracking these on the calendar and for adding them up at the end of the week. He or she can either cash in the points at the end of the day, or save them for a larger reward. This system should be renegotiated every week so that activities reflect the things he or she is currently trying to work toward.

Activities	Points

Points can be exchanged as follows. Overflow points are not lost (for example, if the child or teen gets 55 points in one week and exchanges 50 for a movie, he or she can keep the 5 points for later).

Daily Point Goal: _____ Points

Points	Daily Privileges/Rewards

Weekly Point Goal: _____ Points

Points	Weekly Privileges/Rewards

I agree to put forth my best effort to do the activities that will earn me points.

Child/Teen's Signature: _____

I/We agree to follow the point system to help reward _____ *for reaching his or her goals.*

Parent's/Parents' Signature: _____

Appendix F

Privilege System Worksheet

_____ *will receive privileges for the following activities. This system should be renegotiated every week, so that activities reflect the things he or she is currently trying to work toward.*
I agree to put forth my best effort to do the activities that will earn me privileges.

Activity #1	Privilege

Activity #2	Privilege

Child/Teen's Signature: _____

I/We agree to follow the privilege system to help reward _____ *for reaching his or her goals.*

Parent's/Parents' Signature: _____

Appendix G

Brainstorming Solutions Worksheet

List possible solutions (Be creative!)	Will this solution solve the problem?	Can I really carry it out?	What are the overall effects on me (short and long term)?	What are the overall effects on others (short and long term)?
	Rate (+ = generally positive, − = generally negative, 0 = neutral)			

Resources and Bibliography

Assessment and Management of Pediatric Chronic Pain: Information for Professionals

- Position statement from the American Pain Society (2012). Assessment and management of children with chronic pain. Retrieved from http://www.americanpainsociety.org/uploads/pdfs/aps12-pcp.pdf
- Palermo, Tonya M. (2012). *Cognitive-Behavioral Therapy for Chronic Pain in Children and Adolescents*. New York: Oxford University Press. This is a guide on CBT for clinicians.
- Institute of Medicine. (2011). Relieving pain in America: A blueprint for transforming prevention, care, education and research. Washington DC: National Academic Press. Retrieved from http://www.iom.edu/Reports/2011/Relieving-Pain-in-America-A-Blueprint-for-Transforming-Prevention-Care-Education-Research/Report-Brief.aspx

Assessment and Management of Pediatric Chronic Pain: Books for Parents

- Zeltzer, Lonnie K., & Schlank, Christina B. (2005). *Conquering Your Child's Chronic Pain: A Pediatrician's Guide for Reclaiming a Normal Childhood.* New York: HarperCollins Publishers.
- Krane, Elliot J., & Mitchell, Deborah. (2005). *Relieve Your Child's Chronic Pain: A Doctor's Program for Easing Headaches, Abdominal Pain, Fibromyalgia, Juvenile Rheumatoid Arthritis, and More.* New York: Fireside.

Children's Sleep

- The American Academy of Sleep Medicine, at http://www .aasmnet.org, offers sleep-wellness booklets.
- The National Sleep Foundation (NSF), at http://www.sleepfoun-dation.org, has information on sleep in children and teens.
- The NSF conducts regular polls, called Sleep in America. The poll conducted in 2006 contains information about sleep in teens. See 2006 Sleep in America Poll. Retrieved from http://www.sleepfoun-dation.org/sites/default/files/2006_summary_of_findings.pdf

Relaxation Strategies

- Audio recordings of relaxation skills introduced in this book can be found at http://www.seattlechildrens.org/research/child-health-behavior-and-development/palermo-lab/selected-recent-publications/

Problem-Solving Strategies

- The strategies taught in Chapter 8 are based on those in a book by Arthur Nezu, Christine Nezu, and Thomas D'Zurilla (2006). *Solving Life's Problems: A 5-Step Guide to Enhanced Well-Being.* New York: Springer.

Index